Lost Communities,
Living Memories

DEAR BRUCE,

MANY THANKS FOR HOSTING MY VISIT, YOUR SUPPORT AND THE WARM HOSPITALITY. HOPE YOU FIND THE BOOK TO BE BOTH USEFUL AND MEANINGFUL. BEST WISHES

Lost Communities, Living Memories

Remembering Forced Removals in Cape Town

Edited by Sean Field
Centre for Popular Memory
University of Cape Town

David Philip • Cape Town

This book is dedicated to all those
who experienced forced removals in
Cape Town and beyond

First published in 2001 by
David Philip Publishers (Pty) Ltd,
208 Werdmuller Centre, Claremont 7708, South Africa

ISBN 0-86486-499-X

Designed by *Abdul Amien*
Reproduction by *Imvakalelo Repro*
Printed in South Africa by *CTP Printers*

Acknowledgements:
The authors and publishers would like to thank the following for their
assistance and for permission to reproduce photographic material:
District Six Museum – *Margaux Jordan, Haajirah Esau, Sandy Prosalendis*
Patricia and *Don Pinnock* – Photographs by *Don Pinnock* reprinted
by permission of African Sun Press, P.O. Box 16415,
Vlaeberg 8018, Cape Town
Simon's Town Museum – *Cathrynne May Salter-Jansen* and *Jean le Roux*
South African Library, Cape Town – *Najwa Hendrickse*
University of Cape Town Libraries, Department of Manuscripts and
Archives – *Jasmin Mohamed* and *Lesley Hart*
Land Information Branch, City of Cape Town – *Ian Black*
Cartographer – *Anne Westoby*

Contents

Contributors

Vivian Bickford-Smith: I was born and brought up in Britain. I first visited Cape Town in the 1970s and came across this extraordinary mixture of beautiful geography and dreadful social engineering. My desire to understand the roots of division and discrimination in Cape Town was given particular urgency by the urban uprising of 1976. Becoming an urban historian was about trying to explain the city's present through studying its past. This is a story of human experience. The collection and dissemination of oral history is a crucial part of its retelling.

Sean Field: My passion for oral history is rooted in my family background. During my childhood in Cape Town, everyone in my family spoke a lot, but most were afraid of writing. I was the observant listener with dreams of becoming a writer. It is not surprising that years later, while at university, I became fascinated with doing oral history interviewing. This style of research attracted me because it offered opportunities to speak to, and learn from, working-class people. Oral history also offered the possibility of making a difference in people's lives. Writing and editing the chapters of this book has been tough but rewarding. In the future I want to put more energy into recording oral histories on video and developing films for public audiences.

Michele Paulse: While I enjoy oral history, I find it difficult to work with oral history text and write a history that represents the range of stories that people tell. I credit my mother for my interest in life stories. In our house in Vancouver, Canada, at the kitchen table, as she sewed, prepared a meal or rested between jobs, my mother often spoke of her youth in Swartdam, Athlone. My parents emigrated from Cape Town to Vancouver in 1968. When I lived in Toronto, I researched District Six for an undergraduate course, and in 1991 someone mentioned Tramway Road. The name of the road did not mean anything to me then, and I thought no more of the street. Two months after I returned to Cape Town, one evening in 1997, I drove through Sea Point with my friend Vincent Kolbe. As we drove along Regent Road, I spotted the signpost 'Tramway Road'. I decided to do life history interviews with ex-residents for a doctoral thesis.

Felicity Swanson: My work as a researcher for the WCOHP has involved cataloguing over 600 interviews in our sound archive. A number of these collections contain stories about forced removals in Cape Town. While District Six remains an important part of this history, many other communities were affected, yet are marginalised in public history. I have been involved in writing two articles for this book. The one on District Six should add to an extensive body of work in this area. I hope that the second article on lower Claremont will stimulate the production of new knowledge about forced removals so that new kinds of public history can emerge.

Albert Thomas: Until my retirement at the end of 1993 I was Head of the Student Advice Office of the University of Cape Town. After retirement I conducted oral history research. I am also known as a theatre director, having been involved in community theatre groups for a long time. Since the 1950s I helped to pioneer the plays of German playwright Bertolt Brecht in South Africa. I was born in Simon's Town and was also a victim of the forced removals of people to Ocean View during the 1960s and 1970s. Currently I am the Chairperson of the Return to Simon's Town Committee, which is spearheading the resettling of the people back there. As a resident of Ocean View I daily meet those who, like me, were forced to move. Often our discussions end with the question 'When are we going back to Simon's Town?'

Foreword

While working at the District Six Museum I often encountered visitors from abroad who shared their experiences of forced removals in cities such as Buenos Aries, Glasgow, Boston and Helsinki. The victims were usually rehoused in conditions of vulnerability and containment. They experienced a strong sense of loss in terms of freedom of movement and association, accessibility to diverse options and, most of all, political power. Victims of forced removals in Cape Town experienced the same sense of loss. Cape Town the mother city has traditionally been, on the one hand, a haven for displaced people. On the other hand, it is shamed by its own history of forced removals before and during apartheid.

I really enjoyed this book and hope that it encourages other communities, such as Kalk Bay, Green Point, Protea Village and many others, to record their memories as well. The motives behind, the impact of, and the whole range of responses to forced removals in Cape Town yield a far more complex picture than that which is commonly assumed. It is often forgotten that it was precisely the culturally mixed communities of Cape Town that were a threat to the apartheid government and its white exclusivity. The authors of this book, some of whom personally experienced forced removals, explore these themes within several Cape communities.

Lost Communities, Living Memories is an important contribution to our understanding of popular memory. In addition, it is a very useful training handbook for students of oral history. The power of popular memory may go a long way toward ensuring that, as former President Mandela said, 'this must never, never happen again'.

Vincent Kolbe

Preface

This book is for the survivors of forced removals in Cape Town and their descendants. However, we hope that all Capetonians and visitors to Cape Town will find it interesting and informative. The book was originally researched and written by the Western Cape Oral History Project (WCOHP). The project was launched in 1984 and was renamed and reconceptualised as the Centre for Popular Memory (CPM) early in 2001. The CPM is based at the University of Cape Town (UCT).

The CPM has five areas of activity. First, we conduct oral history and other memory projects. Second, oral histories are passed on through popular history mediums such as books and exhibitions, and in time we will be using radio and film. Third, an internship programme trains students and members of community organisations in oral history interviewing and archival skills. Fourth, we manage a public audio-visual archive of over 600 oral history interviews, including interviews with dockworkers, domestic workers, political activists and residents from different Cape Town communities. Finally, we develop local and international partnerships with organisations such as the District Six Museum in Cape Town and the Matrix Centre at Michigan State University.

The writing and editing of this book took approximately three years to complete. The oral histories quoted in this book were recorded by various researchers since the mid-1980s. Through this lengthy process, there have been many, many people who have helped in direct and indirect ways. Therefore, not everyone can be mentioned by name; nevertheless, we would like to express our sincere gratitude to all who were involved in this project in any way.

Most importantly, we sincerely thank all those who were interviewed, who gave us their time, energy and memories. Unfortunately, a book of this kind can only quote from a small number of the thousands of stories that were recorded. The stories that were not used in this book are certainly not unimportant and can be heard at the CPM's audio-visual archive.

The CPM is indebted to Professor Bill Nasson and Professor Vivian Bickford-Smith for their guidance. Many thanks also go to the various staff members of the Historical Studies Department at UCT and to our colleagues in the History Department at the University of the Western Cape (UWC), who have supported us over the years.

Our core funders have been the National Research Foundation, the Swiss Agency for Development and Cooperation and the Anglo American Chairman's Fund Educational Trust. Without their funding to the WCOHP and now the CPM, this book would not have been possible. The Cultural Affairs Committee of the Cape Town City Council and the Standard Bank Foundation have also generously donated funds towards the publication of this book.

We would also like to thank all the authors and their partners, families and friends for supporting them through the difficulties of writing and rewriting. To my partner, Jane van der Riet, I am indebted to you beyond words. A special thank you goes to Felicity Swanson, my research assistant, who did most of the copy-editing and wrote two of the chapters. And finally I would like to thank Carohn Cornell, who helped us to write clearly and accessibly.

In recent times it is often glibly stated that 'Cape Town is not an African city'. This statement crudely manipulates observations of racialised spaces and places in the city to arrive at an a historical, essentialist conclusion. Cape Town is an African city and like most African cities it has a hybrid social and cultural formation. The city and its rural hinterland have been shaped by the painful exclusion and oppression of people classified 'African' and 'coloured' by colonial, segregationist and apartheid regimes. Forced removals were a significant aspect of the making of Cape Town, and both their effects and affects are still evident today. We hope this book will move people to think about the oral histories and popular memories that make up Cape Town's brutal yet dynamic past.

Sean Field

1 Oral Histories of Forced Removals

Sean Field

When people speak about their memories, evocative oral histories are created and expressed. Imagine yourself in the shoes of this storyteller:

> Oh! Don't talk to me about that, please don't talk to me. I will cry. I will cry all over again. There's when the trouble started. When they chuck us out like that. When they chucked us out of Cape Town. My whole life became changed! There was change. Not just in me, but in all the people. What they took away they can never give it back to us again [weeps]. Oh! I want to cry so much, all over again … I cannot explain how it was when I moved out of Cape Town and I came to Manenberg. In those days I didn't know why they chuck us out. What did we do, that they chuck us out like this? We wasn't murderers, we wasn't robbers, like today. Now people are corrupt. They can really be barbarians. They murder one another and that is what they wanted … It was wrong what the white people did. These people did wrong. They had everything, everything that a person's heart yearns for. And we had nothing but we were satisfied. They broke us up. They broke up the community. They took our happiness from us. The day they threw us out of Cape Town, that was my whole life tumbling down. I don't know how my life continued. I couldn't see my life in this raw township far away from the family. All the neighbours were strangers. That was the hardest part of my life, believe me. (Mrs G.J., former resident of District Six)[1]

Mrs G.J.'s story and her feelings of loss, sadness and anger are difficult to ignore. But thousands of people who experienced forced removals in South Africa have been ignored, silenced or forgotten. Between 1913 and 1983, it is estimated that at least 3,9 million people were forcibly removed in South Africa.[2] The apartheid government and previous governments used various racist laws, such as pass laws and the Group Areas Act of 1950, to forcibly remove people from their communities. Mrs G.J. asks questions about why forced removals happened and how forced removals changed people's lives. By drawing on and interpreting oral histories this book will explore these central questions. We hope it will contribute to the recorded memory of forced removals and help present and future generations to learn more about the impact of forced removals on the city of Cape Town.

This is not 'the whole story' of forced removals in Cape Town. But it is an introduction to the topic and to the stories of District Six, Windermere, Tramway Road, Simon's Town and lower Claremont. How these communities were destroyed or transformed through forced removals and how and why former residents keep their memories alive are the threads that connect these stories.

Listening to Oral Histories

> There was no escaping that. And if you forgot your pass, it's either you had to outrun the police or you got arrested. And, uh, it was, that was one sad error … the van would sort

of just appear [he claps hands] from nowhere and before it's stationary the police are off and you would run. You know it was so pathetic that sometimes a person would run and after he discover that, 'I got my pass on me'. Ahee! So it was, I won't be able to, to paint a fairer picture it was such a nightmare thing. It was such a nightmare thing. (Mr I.Z.)[3]

The words we speak are usually fluid because they do not have to obey the rules of grammar and spelling like written words. When spoken words are written down they often look unusual and ungrammatical.[4] It does not matter where you come from, which language you speak, or how educated you are, when your spoken words are turned into written words they look untidy. But this untidiness is a strength, which reveals clues about how people remember and talk about the past. Mr I.Z. chose particular words to describe his personal memories of pass law raids in Windermere of the 1950s. But he also constructed these sentences and stories to convey a set of shared memories felt by others.

Recording oral history is usually not about famous people or leaders. Rather, popular and public forms of oral history aim to include everyone's past, especially the past of those who have been oppressed, marginalised or forgotten. The unnoticed makers of history also want to be acknowledged and remembered. The Group Areas Act, pass laws and many other apartheid laws and racist ideologies undermined how people feel about themselves and their histories. Many potential interviewees argue with interviewers that their lives are 'unimportant', 'uninteresting', or that they have 'nothing useful to say'. Oral and popular historians (and others involved in communities) have a role to play in convincing people that they have meaningful pasts and valuable lives.

It is sometimes claimed that ordinary people are voiceless. This is not true. People do have voices and they do speak out. Rather, the problem is: do they have sufficiently strong public voices and, most crucially, who is listening to them? Who will listen to or bear witness to the thousands who

want to tell their stories about life under apartheid? The Truth and Reconciliation Commission (TRC) has done significant work in recording and publicising the stories of people who suffered 'horrendous human rights abuses'.[5] But what about the millions who fall outside the narrow focus of the TRC? What about the people who had their human rights abused through forced removals? What about the perpetrators of forced removals? These are questions this book cannot answer, but they are questions that need to be asked. In most societies, including the new South Africa, it is people with financial and political resources who have more opportunities to present their stories to the relevant authorities and broader public audiences. By contrast, it is the stories of the economically poor and politically marginalised that are not listened to.

Historically, oral history projects have played a role in recording the stories of marginalised groups in society, but these projects have limited staff, resources and funding. These projects cannot rescue people from their socio-economic problems or emotional traumas, but they can disseminate people's stories to many public audiences. As will be explored in Chapter 8, by listening to, recording and disseminating oral histories, small but significant contributions can be made to healing and development in South Africa.

Stories in Word and Image

The chapters that follow are formed by stories constructed through oral testimonies and photographs. The central aim of this book is to demonstrate the compelling power of oral and visual histories, which represent the memories of people who went through the dislocation, dispersal and pain of forced removals.

Chapter 2 provides some general background information on forced removals in the Western Cape. It breaks down several myths about Cape Town before the National Party came to power in 1948. For example, forced removals were conducted in the city long before the onset of apartheid government. Vivian Bickford-Smith outlines how the apartheid government aimed to make the region a haven for people classified white and coloured only. The removals of Africans through influx control measures and Group Areas Act removals are described. Apartheid planners did not fully succeed in implementing their nightmare plan. But the social and spatial map of the city was dramatically reshaped by their racist social engineering and the responses of residents and community organisations.

Chapter 3 tells the story of the rise of Windermere in the early part of the twentieth century and how it was destroyed by the forced removals of the apartheid state in the late 1950s to early 1960s. The Windermere community was culturally mixed, and comprised coloured, African and white residents. It was mainly a squatter community, emerging on the margins of the urban centre of the city. It was situated in a semi-rural landscape of bushes and characterised by pools of water and livestock. Windermere–Kensington was declared a coloured group area in 1958. Residents classified African, white and Asian were forcibly removed. The ways people remember community life in Windermere and how they were forcibly removed are interpreted.

In Chapter 4, Michele Paulse describes the Tramway Road community and how this small pocket of homes, occupied mostly by coloured people, was surrounded by the mainly white Sea Point community. Tramway Road was an intimate community of families who worked, played and lived together. Their closeness reinforced a sense of community identity. But the community also experienced internal differences, which were influenced by the world beyond the social and physical boundaries of Tramway Road. When the area was classified white and people were removed from Tramway Road and nearby Ilford Road, it was like a family being torn apart. In recent times these residents have reunited to remember the past and demand restitution for their losses.

Much has been said and written about District Six, but in Chapter 5 Felicity Swanson and Jane Harries explore a broader range of memories about community life in District Six. For example, the repeated description of life being 'all wonder-

ful' is revealed to be only one version of how life was experienced and remembered. The area was classified white because of the value of inner-city property and the political problem of a multi-cultural suburb on the doorstep of the city centre. The suffering of ex-District Six residents has been publicised through various popular mediums, such as books and musicals. Significantly, it is the District Six story that has symbolically come to represent the plight of all people who were forcibly removed in Cape Town.

In Chapter 6, Albert Thomas, an ex-resident of Simon's Town, writes about this culturally mixed community of residents classified white, coloured and African. This chapter starts with an historical background to the growth of this seaside and naval town. Under the Group Areas Act it was declared a white area and the coloured residents of Simon's Town and the African residents of Luyolo township were forcibly removed to places like Ocean View and Guguletu. This chapter also highlights the importance of various religious, sports and cultural organisations, and ends by interpreting the social cost of forced removals and the difficulties of settling into Ocean View.

The memories of the residents of lower Claremont, below the southern suburbs railway line, form the heart of Chapter 7. Felicity Swanson weaves together residents' stories about gangs, the Coon Carnival and other cultural activities. People who lived in the area popularly know as *die Vlak* developed a strong sense of community belonging. The community was declared a white area in 1967 and then renamed Harfield Village. This racial zoning occurred much later here than in other southern suburbs communities, but the social and emotional costs of forced removals were tragically similar.

The final chapter explores the fundamental issues of restitution, memory, living heritage and how oral history can contribute to healing and development. In closing, it argues that oral history has a role to play in deepening democracy in South Africa.

The appendix, aimed at students of oral his-tory, contains a flexible, practical step-by-step guide to conducting an oral history project. While recording oral history requires time, energy and resources, it can be done by nearly anyone. If this book stimulates people to record oral histories and to pass on these stories to others, then it will have served a very useful function.

In general terms, we argue that oral, visual and other historians need to resist attempts to enclose the past in some grand or official casket. The past is always open to different interpretations, new disclosures and political contestation. Therefore, this book is opposed to old and new forms of silencing or manipulating the past.

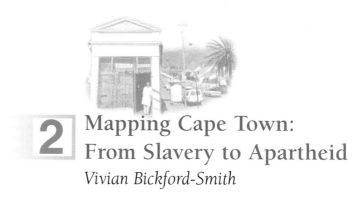

2 | Mapping Cape Town: From Slavery to Apartheid

Vivian Bickford-Smith

This chapter challenges a number of myths about the history of Cape Town before the National Party government came to power in 1948. The chapter then looks at the period from 1948 when apartheid was extended to every aspect of people's lives.

The first myth is that Africans are newcomers in Cape Town and do not belong here. The chapter traces the forgotten history of African Capetonians.

A second myth is that there was no segregation in Cape Town before the National Party government introduced its apartheid policy from 1948. In fact, segregation was in place in Cape Town long before this time. In the 1880s and 1890s, for instance, some areas of Cape Town were by law for whites only, and there was informal segregation in some other areas.

According to another myth, forced removals first happened in the 1950s under the Group Areas Act. In reality, Cape Town's first forced removals took place fifty years earlier. In 1901, Africans living in District Six and elsewhere in the city were forced to move to barracks in the docks and to Ndabeni location, far from the city.

The chapter also shows how from 1948 the National Party government extended apartheid to every aspect of people's lives. The Group Areas Act forced people of different racial groups to live in separate areas. When an area was classified white, people classified coloured were forced to move even if their families had lived there for generations. Other chapters in this book focus on some of the communities which

suffered forced removals in Cape Town in the 1950s and early 1960s.

Cape Town during the Time of Slavery: 1652–1838

When European settlers arrived, the Cape was peopled by groups of herders known as the Khoi. The Khoi did not want to give up their independent way of life to work for the settlers, and the Dutch East India Company forbade its officials to enslave the local people. The Cape began importing slaves, who soon outnumbered the settlers.[1]

From the 1650s to the 1830s it was the slaves who did most of the work at the Cape. They were builders and carpenters, gardeners and farm workers, fishermen, coachmen, tailors, domestic servants. The old Slave Lodge of the Dutch East India Company still stands next to the Company Gardens in Cape Town. Private owners kept slaves all over the city, in the towns and on the farms of the Boland and in the outlying areas. Some freed slaves, both men and women, became prominent in the life of the Cape, but we know very little about the lives of the vast majority.

The economy depended on slave labour. Slaves also contributed to the language and culture of the Cape. One scholar has described Afrikaans as 'the language the slaves made'.[2] Many slaves – including African slaves – were Muslim or became Muslim and are among the ancestors of the Cape Muslims. There are also Christian communities, like Pniel or St Philip's in District Six, which honour Christian slaves and freed slaves among their ancestors.

There is a common belief that the slaves all came from the East Indies, but research shows that slaves came from all around the Indian Ocean.[3] Most of those who came to the Cape were from East Africa, Madagascar and the Indian subcontinent or the East Indies, and small numbers came from Angola and West Africa. Thousands of their descendants were born into slavery at the Cape.

After the Slaves were Freed: 1838 to the 1890s

Slavery was abolished in three stages. In 1807 the British banned the slave trade, so no more slaves could be imported to the Cape. In 1834 slavery was abolished and slaves were freed but they had to work for their old owners as so-called apprentices until 1838.

From then on, all men, black or white, were supposed to be equal before the law. All men (but no women) had the right to vote in local and central government elections – but only if they earned a certain wage or owned property. In Cape Town society in the middle of the 1800s, an individual's status depended more on wealth and gender than on race. Almost all of the rich and powerful were white, or considered themselves white, but the poor included people of all colours.

From the 1830s large numbers of Xhosa-speaking people lived in Cape Town. Some settled permanently while others remained migrant workers. Many were refugees from the wars on the eastern frontier. The first to settle and find work in Cape Town were hundreds of Mfengu from the Eastern Cape, some with wives and families. People were also forced to come to Cape Town from the Eastern Cape after the cattle killing of 1857. The 1865 census recorded about 700 'Kafirs' in Papendorp (present-day Woodstock) and Cape Town, apart from prisoners on Robben Island. By 1900 there were about 1 500 dock-workers in the harbour barracks and about 8 000

'Natives' living elsewhere in the city, mostly in District Six.

The Cape Town City Council employed Africans as street cleaners, at the Strand Street quarry and at the reservoirs on the mountain. Others worked as labourers for builders, coal merchants, the brick-fields or the tramways, or as office messengers and cleaners. Xhosa-speaking people were very much part of Cape Town and other areas in the Western Cape.[4]

From Slavery to Segregation

In the 1880s and 1890s many powerful whites came to believe that segregation was a good idea. They were influenced by false theories about inferior and superior races.[5] There were some whites who spoke out against racism, but by 1901 many 'were urging that, as in the southern United States, blacks – coloureds as well as Africans – in Cape Town should be barred from trams, cabs and even sidewalks'.[6]

At the time some black (coloured and African) men had the right to vote in elections for local government and for the Cape Parliament. To keep them in the minority, powerful whites made it harder for blacks to qualify as voters. Few blacks earned enough money or owned enough property to vote. Communally owned land did not count.

It became official policy to separate whites and blacks in government institutions like hospitals, jails and schools. Sometimes this policy was enforced by law. Many privately owned facilities like theatres and bars, as well as sports teams, also became segregated. But it was more difficult to segregate residential areas. Since the 1840s most of Cape Town's lower-class areas had been racially mixed. Whites, coloureds and Africans were neighbours. This included Kanaladorp, later known as District Six. It was far too expensive to build segregated areas. In 1891 the Editor of the *Cape Argus* commented that in Cape Town it was 'now too late to separate the white and coloured population as should have been done from the first'.[7]

Cape Town's First Forced Removal

Africans were an easier target than coloureds for residential segregation. By 1900 they made up about 10 000 of Cape Town's total population of about 160 000 and there was talk of a 'Kafir invasion'. The Prime Minister of the Cape Colony, W.P. Schreiner, believed that Africans did not really belong in Cape Town, although the city needed their labour:

> We have in the neighbourhood of Cape Town some 10 000 raw natives. They live all over the place and they are learning all sorts of bad habits through living in touch with European and coloured surroundings. We cannot get rid of them, they are necessary for work, what we want is to get them practically in the position of being compounded. Keep the natives out of harm's way, let them do their work, receive their wages and at the end of their term let them go back to the place whence they came, to the native territories.[8]

The compound system had been developed by the mining companies in Kimberley and on the Witwatersrand to control African workers. The workers were forced to live in crowded dormitories in compounds, which were tightly supervised. They were not allowed to bring their families with them. The Prime Minister wanted Cape Town to have compounds to segregate Africans and control their lives.

The excuse for the first forced removal was the deadly bubonic plague which hit Cape Town in 1901 during the Anglo–Boer War. The disease was carried by fleas on rats in the hay that was imported from Argentina to feed the British horses. African dockworkers who unloaded the hay were among the plague's first victims, and as a result the health authorities blamed Africans for spreading

An unknown woman is arrested as an 'illegal resident' in Cape Town for not having a pass book in her possession

(Black Sash Archives, University of Cape Town Libraries/Manuscripts and Archives)

the disease. Cape government officials used the Public Health Amendment Act of 1897 to force Africans into locations.[9]

Most were forced into two locations: a barracks at the docks and another at Uitvlugt forest station (soon renamed Ndabeni) near modern-day Pinelands. The town guard was called out to round up Africans and herd them to the station. Sam Ntungwana recalled:

I had my goods packed up ready to be loaded ... The soldiers came to me in the afternoon. They told me to bring back all the things which I had already taken out. I locked the room. After three days I went back to bring my things. I could not find them. I was told that they were burned.[10]

The location was enclosed by a six-foot-high barbed wire fence and guards checked the identity cards of residents. There were five big corrugated iron huts, each sleeping about five hundred people, and about six hundred small iron shacks for families or small groups of men. The area was muddy, windy and flooded in winter. The new location was not a healthy place to live. There were outbreaks of typhoid, cholera, bronchitis and pneumonia. The underlying reasons for the forced removal were white racism and the desire to control African workers.

African Resistance to Forced Removals

The history of resistance to these early forced removals makes interesting reading. Some people refused to move from their homes in the city and were forced out, losing their property. Others merged into the coloured population. Many people voted with their feet: they went back to the rural areas rather than be forced to live in a location. African Capetonians were already using struggle tactics that became famous much later. There was resistance to carrying 'plague passes'. There were strikes and stayaways, mass meetings on the Grand Parade and

on the slopes of the mountain, a protest march of a thousand men. The forced removals went ahead but the residents won a few concessions. For instance, the ban on leaving the location on foot was lifted.

Health regulations gave the authorities emergency powers for three months. When this time had elapsed the residents protested that they were being held in Ndabeni unlawfully and staged a work stayaway. There were court appeals and petitions and delegations to the Cape authorities and later also to the British government.

A newspaper editor who visited Ndabeni reported that most of the residents regarded the removal as oppression. After the Prime Minister visited Ndabeni he reported that nobody had ever spoken to him as strongly as the people he met there.[11] A prominent leader of the resistance was Alfred Mangena, a young man who later qualified as an advocate in London and on his return to South Africa joined the African National Congress (ANC) in 1912. Before he went overseas, Mangena addressed a mass meeting in Ndabeni. He called on people to continue their rent boycott and to boycott train fares, saying: 'If you are prevented from travelling on the trains you must not go to work'.[12]

Residents who appeared in court justified the rent and fare boycott on the grounds that they were being kept prisoner in the location. Their defence lawyer argued that they were being kept in huts unfit for the accommodation of pigs. But they were found guilty and fined.

Twenty-five years later there was a second forced removal. Ndabeni location was taken over from the government by the Cape Town municipality. As the city grew, the authorities wanted Ndabeni as an industrial site next to Ndabeni Station. Despite protests, the location was demolished and residents were moved to Langa, three miles further from the city centre and beyond the white suburbs. The people of Ndabeni lost their homes, their schools and their churches and had to start again in Langa. '"The place of talk" had become the place of silence.'[13]

Locations and Shantytowns

After the plague had passed, the Cape government passed the Native Reserve Locations Act of 1902. This gave the government the power to force urban Africans to live in locations. The only people allowed to live outside locations were domestic servants, registered voters and those with special permission. But many others chose to defy the law.

In 1910 the Cape joined the other three provinces to form the Union of South Africa. This meant that Africans at the Cape were subject to new national laws. The Natives (Urban Areas) Act of 1923 laid down that all Africans should be seg-

regated in locations. There was also tighter control over Africans moving to towns and cities, which became known as 'influx control'.

From 1937 Africans were forbidden to buy land outside the reserves, except from other Africans. Men who came to town from the rural areas had to get official permission to look for work. If they did not find work within a short time, they could be ordered to leave town. The authorities also had the power to ban from town anyone they considered to be living 'an idle, dis-

Canterbury flats, District Six, 1938

(South African Library)

solute or disorderly life'.[14] Anyone who employed an African man had to register his employment contract and pay a fee. A small number of Africans were exempted from these laws and free to live in town: those on the voters' roll, those who owned land, chiefs, clergymen and some teachers. Influx control did not apply to women but at that time few African women lived in urban areas.[15]

It was difficult to enforce influx control in the Cape Peninsula. One reason was that there were so many separate authorities. The Cape Town City Council had authority over part of the Peninsula, but areas like Simon's Town and Wynberg had their own separate local councils. Most of the Peninsula was still rural and the Cape Divisional Council was in charge of the more rural areas like Retreat and Windermere. The Divisional Council did not have enough officials to police these areas, so people built more and more shacks. The Divisional Council did not want to demolish

shacks once the roof was on, in case they had to give people accommodation.

During the Second World War many more Africans came to work in Cape Town and influx control was temporarily relaxed. After the war, influx control was re-imposed on African men. It still did not apply to African women. The Peninsula and the Cape Flats came under the control of the Divisional Council. There were more officials to raid for 'illegals' and force them to leave the urban areas. The plan was to keep Africans out of the Western Cape as far as possible.[16]

At the same time railway authorities in the Eastern Cape were given the power to stop Africans from travelling to Cape Town. Cape Town employers had to pay the costs of sending Africans home at the end of their contracts. This was to make sure that migrant workers did not stay in town and to discourage employers from employing Africans. These laws and regulations were designed to keep Africans out of the towns, or in

Apartheid signs

(District Six Museum)

separate locations at the edge of the towns. But they did not succeed. In 1948 about 80 per cent of Africans were living outside the locations, despite these laws. They lived in different parts of the Peninsula, some in formal housing, most in shantytowns.[17]

Segregated Coloured Areas before 1948

Before 1948 only Africans were forced by law to live in segregated areas but separate white and coloured areas were also developing. For a long time richer whites had been buying houses on big plots in suburbs like Kenilworth, Claremont and Rondebosch, which were too expensive for most coloured people. The result was residential segregation, even if it was not planned that way. Most coloureds in the suburbs were on smaller properties in coloured pockets set apart from whites. Tramway Road in Sea Point or Harfield Village in Claremont are examples. These coloured pockets provided labour for the surrounding white areas.

By 1900 some richer white areas like Milnerton, Oranjezicht and parts of Camps Bay had clauses in all title deeds to keep out coloureds and Africans. In 1894 the Editor of the *Cape Argus* wrote that he hoped whites would all move out to these areas or to the southern suburbs, leaving inner Cape Town to be a coloured location.[18] Over the next fifty years the Editor's dream almost came true.

There were a number of factors in favour of segregated areas. Free compulsory education for poor whites made it possible for more people to move into whites-only areas. So did municipal housing schemes. In the 1920s and 1930s, the Cape Town City Council built low-cost housing for the poor of all races. The Council was careful to keep coloured housing at a distance from white areas. Maitland Garden Village, Bokmakierie, Silvertown and Kew Town were for coloureds only. Brooklyn and Epping Garden Village were for whites.

The Slums Act of 1934 gave municipalities the power to redevelop any area they considered a slum. The Cape Town City Council demolished many 'slum' buildings in District Six and built over a thousand new homes for coloureds only. For example, residents of Well's Square in the heart of District Six were moved to the newly built Bloemhof–Canterbury flats below De Waal Drive.

In 1938 and 1939 the Cape provincial government and Parliament both tried to pass laws to enforce coloured residential segregation. They failed, mainly because of massive protests led by Cissie Gool and other members of the National

'Whites only' sign in a children's playground

(Black Sash Archives, University of Cape Town Libraries/Manuscripts and Archives)

Separate entrances for whites and blacks at a post office

(Black Sash Archives, University of Cape Town Libraries/Manuscripts
and Archives)

Liberation League. The move to segregation was interrupted by the beginning of the Second World War in 1939. But at the end of the war, when local councils and provincial and national government built housing, areas were segregated.

Flats were built for coloured fishermen in Kalk Bay and semi-detached cottages were built in Hout Bay. Flats and cottages in Milnerton and Plumstead were for white ex-soldiers only. The government packages for white ex-soldiers helped many to buy houses in suburbs like Meadowridge and Bergvliet, which had whites-only title deeds.[19] The same was true for Vredehoek, upper Woodstock, Pinelands, Rondebosch, and Fish Hoek.[20] Coloureds who could afford to buy in these areas were kept out by whites-only title deeds, so they moved into houses in areas like Athlone or Crawford. The poor moved into shacks in areas like Windermere or squatter camps between Bellville and Retreat.[21]

This meant that many areas of Cape Town were segregated before 1948. But there were exceptions. Cissie Gool lived in Vredehoek and shared a beach cottage in Camps Bay with her parents, the Abdurahmans, although this upset some of their white neighbours.[22] There were still a few mixed residential areas with white and coloured residents. These were mainly in the old inner-city areas of Mowbray, Salt River and Woodstock. There were also mixed communities where Africans and Indians lived amongst the mainly coloured residents, in areas like District Six, Tramway Road or lower Claremont. Both coloureds and Africans lived in shack areas like Windermere and the Blouvlei settlement in Retreat.[23]

The Group Areas Act: Redrawing the Map of Cape Town

It is clear that segregation and removals were a reality in Cape Town long before the apartheid policy was formulated. But what was new about apartheid? The Population Registration Act of 1950 officially divided South Africans into four groups: 'whites', 'coloureds', 'Asians' and 'Natives' and required them to register accordingly. There were even 'race inspectors' to decide difficult cases. This opened the way for more complete segregation in Cape Town. Marriages and relationships between black and white became illegal. Other laws aimed to segregate schools and universities, political organisations, buses and trains and taxis, ambulances and hospital wards, sport and music, restaurants and theatres, parks and beaches, benches and public toilets, libraries and post offices, even graveyards.

The Group Areas Act of 1950 aimed to stop mixed residential areas in South African cities. From 1951 the government took control of all property transfers and changes of occupancy that went across racial lines. By law owners were not allowed to sell or rent property to people of the wrong racial group. The system was administered by the Land Tenure Advisory Board (LTAB), later renamed the Group Areas Board.

Some municipalities such as Bellville, Goodwood and Parow were controlled by the National Party. They helped the Board by drawing up plans for separate racial zoning in their areas. The municipality of Cape Town refused to co-operate but that did not stop the Board from deciding on racial zones for Cape Town.

To understand how Group Areas removals were planned, it is useful to know the railway lines that start from the city. The Board proposed that railway lines should be used to separate white areas from coloured and black African areas. The plan was to move all blacks south of the Bellville line and east of the Simon's Town line. Even more blacks were to be removed from the area between the Simon's Town and Cape Flats lines. The only exceptions were domestic servants who were needed in white homes.

These proposals were discussed at public hearings in 1956. Radical individuals and organisations boycotted the proceedings. The Board made only a few concessions, such as zoning lower Wynberg for coloureds, and went ahead with its plans. The first areas to be proclaimed in 1957/8 were those in the northern suburbs and those with fewest 'disqualified people' like Parow and Bellville. Black residents of Tramway Road

were told they were living in a white group area; Windermere Africans in a coloured one. Later District Six and the coloured 'pockets' of Claremont were declared white.

If you were the wrong race, you were given a specific number of years in which to move. A resident of Black River, Rondebosch, said, 'This is my home – and if they want to get me and my family out of it they will have to bring their tanks and Sten guns.'[24] In the end, little force was needed to remove people from most areas. The time of eviction varied from area to area. There were delays because people could only be forced to move if alternative accommodation was available. However, there was a shortage. By 1962 the Group Areas Board had only built about three hundred houses on the Cape Flats, so it looked as though the delays might continue. But by the end of 1959 the Cape Town City Council decided to make Council housing available to people who had been removed under the Group Areas Act. In fact, Group Areas legislation 'compelled all local councils to set aside at least 40 per cent of all newly constructed homes for removed persons'.[25]

In 1960 – in the middle of a national State

Site C, Khayelitsha location, on the Cape Flats

(Black Sash Archives, University of Cape Town Libraries/Manuscripts and Archives)

of Emergency – the government announced more white areas. The map on page 25 clearly shows the government's strategy. The white areas cover the most valuable property of the inner city and the mountain slopes of the Peninsula. There is usually a barrier between coloured and white areas. Often the barrier is an industrial area – like the massive area of Epping Industria between Bonteheuwel and Pinelands. Sometimes the barrier is a road or railway, or a green belt.

By 1979 the only undecided area was a small part of Woodstock. About 150 000 people had been forcibly removed, the vast majority of them coloured. They were evicted from older residential areas or shack communities and moved to new townships or locations on the Cape Flats. Some of the older areas like Harfield Village in Claremont, Mowbray, and Protea Village near Kirstenbosch were renovated by property developers for whites. But Tramway Road and District Six were demolished. The novelist Richard Rive described this destruction as 'Cape Town's Hiroshima'.

The Apartheid Dream: Removing Africans from Cape Town

In the meantime, the National Party had followed its dream of the Western Cape without any Africans. The new Minister of Native Affairs, Dr E.G. Jansen, said in 1948:

> Whatever claim, morally or otherwise, the Natives have in other parts of the Union, they have no real claim to be here in the Western Province at all. It is within the memory of many people today that there was a time that a Native was unknown in the Peninsula.[26]

To return to an imaginary past in which no Africans lived in Cape Town, the National Party passed two new laws and changed an old law.

Firstly, in 1952 the Prevention of Illegal Squatting Act was applied to greater Cape Town. This Act forced local authorities (municipalities) to

help set up 'emergency camps' where shack dwellers could be 'concentrated and controlled'. The Act also allowed local authorities to demolish 'illegal' shacks even if there was no alternative accommodation. The northern municipalities of Parow and Bellville began to remove African families. They were supposed to move to an extension of Nyanga, a new location. But the Cape Town City Council did not want to act against shack dwellers. There was conflict about whether local or central government would pay for the new housing. The central government ordered the Council to build more housing for male migrant labourers at Langa – but no more family housing. More family housing for Africans was built in the early 1960s in Nyanga West, later renamed Guguletu.

Secondly, in 1952 the Natives (Urban Areas) Act of 1923 was amended in an attempt to prevent Africans coming to the cities. Under Section 10 of this Act, Africans were allowed only three days to look for work and for the first time African women had to get work permits in Cape Town. However, the government had to make a few concessions because employers wanted a more stable workforce and in any case, this policy was too expensive to enforce. African men were given the right to live permanently in the city, but only if they could prove that they had lived in the city continuously since birth or for at least fifteen years, or if they had worked for one employer without a break for ten years. Wives and children of those who benefited from this law also had the right to live in the city.

Thirdly, the so-called 'Natives (Abolition of Passes and Co-ordination of Documents) Act' was also passed in 1952. Every African man over the age of 16 had to carry a reference book with a photograph. Passes, work seekers' permits and work contracts all had to go into this 'domboek' or 'dompas'. As the names show, the reference book was hated and despised. There were more and more pass raids against 'illegals'. For instance, on 1 December 1953 about eight hundred police took part in a massive raid on Windermere, where they arrested two hundred residents.[27] To back up police, location inspectors were granted powers of search and arrest in 1958.

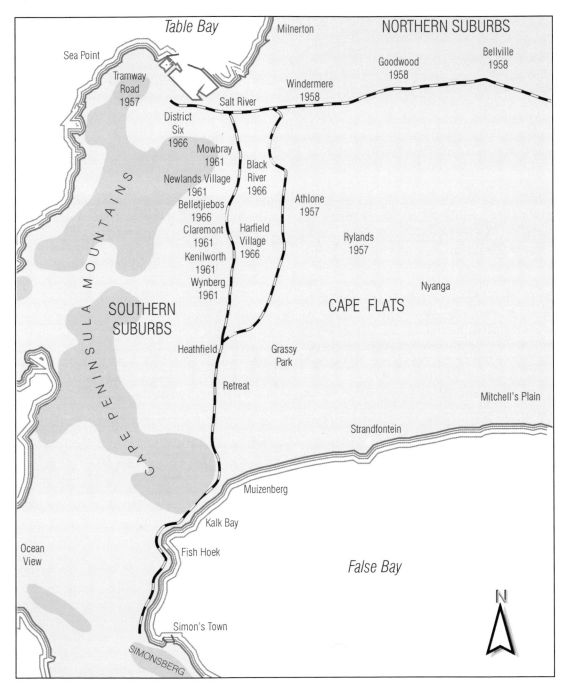

At the same time there were more and more shack clearances, from Hout Bay to Elsies River. 'Bachelors' – many of them married men with families – were ordered into single quarters in the locations and more than seventy new barracks were built at Langa. A Langa resident said, 'Township is not a fit name for the place. It is a compound ... The buildings are like graves.'[28] And at Nyanga West, all the houses built were designed so that they could be converted into single quarters. Africans were not allowed to buy houses but could only take a thirty-year lease. Many were 'endorsed' out of Cape Town altogether: this happened to more than eighteen thousand men and almost six thousand women between 1954 and 1962 alone.[29]

While all this was happening in Cape Town, conditions in the Eastern Cape reserves were getting worse. The situation reached a crisis in 1960. A mass protest against the pass laws, organised by the Pan-Africanist Congress (PAC), was to begin on 21 March. In the morning people tried to march to Langa police station, but the march was called off for fear of violence. An evening meeting was held to report back on the events of the day, a day which had seen 69 protesters killed by police at Sharpeville in the Transvaal. Police dispersed the crowd at the Langa meeting, killing two more people. After a week-long work stayaway, the government declared a State of Emergency on 30 March. There were mass arrests and the PAC and ANC were banned. Opposition seemed to have been crushed.

More attempts followed to remove Africans from the Western Cape. Government control of Africans, now known as Bantu Administration, was tightened. From 1965 African workers had to return to their 'homeland' at the end of each contract period, and re-apply for the job from there. This was to interrupt continuous employment or continuous residence to make sure that no more Africans acquired Section 10 rights to permanent residence. After 1966, the government built no more housing for Africans in Cape Town. By the late 1960s people who were 'endorsed' out of Cape Town were being sent to 'resettlement camps' in the Eastern Cape, and the Bantu Affairs Department could remove Section 10 rights if a person was deemed 'idle' or 'undesirable'.

All these measures were intended to remove Africans from Cape Town, but people were desperate to come to the city, even at the risk of arrest. The official figures show that the African population rose from about 70 000 in 1960 to around 250 000 by 1974 – and the real figures were probably higher.[30] New squatter areas grew, mainly near the airport. The Illegal Squatting Act of 1977 allowed Bantu Affairs officials to demolish shacks without a court order. The squatter areas of Unibel and Modderdam were demolished. Crossroads was also in danger of being demolished in 1977 but was saved for a time by strong community organisation and a Cape Supreme Court order against demolition. International protests put pressure on the government. Later government-backed vigilantes set off civil strife in Crossroads; many homes were burnt down and many people fled the area.[31]

More shack settlements went up at KTC, Nyanga Bush, Portland Cement and elsewhere, as people moved out of the overcrowded townships and more people came to Cape Town from the Eastern Cape. In 1983, Piet Koornhof, Minister of Co-operation and Development, announced the government's new plan. All Africans who had the right to stay in the Cape Peninsula would be moved to a new township, Khayelitsha, between the N2 motorway and False Bay. 'Illegals' would be sent back to their 'homelands'.[32]

This chapter cannot tell the long and complicated story of how apartheid began to break down in Cape Town. Influx control was abandoned in 1986, and the Group Areas Act repealed in 1991. In 1994 the ANC-led democratic government set up a land claims process for people who had lost their homes or land through forced removals under apartheid. The new government also promised houses for millions of people. Some people have benefited from the possibilities of the new era. Most are still waiting.

Did the apartheid planners – and the earlier segregationists – succeed in creating an apartheid city? It looks like it if you take the road or the railway line from the city centre past District Six and Ndabeni, onto the Cape Flats, past Langa to Crossroads and Khayelitsha. The apartheid laws are gone, there are some mixed residential areas, but most Capetonians still live in separate African, coloured and white areas.

3 Windermere: Squatters, Slumyards and Removals, 1920s to 1960s

Sean Field

If you are travelling along the N1 highway from the city centre of Cape Town towards the northern suburbs, you will see the airbase at Ysterplaat on your left. As you move past Ysterplaat, rather turn your eyes right and you will see a railway line and rows of houses. These housing areas are known as the communities of Kensington and Factreton today (see map on page 28). Before the mid-1960s the areas were known as Windermere and Kensington.

The residents of the Windermere–Kensington community lived in both brick houses and iron shanties. By the 1920s, the majority of residents were living in shanties, and by the 1940s, Windermere had become Cape Town's largest squatter settlement.[1] It was a culturally vibrant but economically poor community. People classified as African, coloured and white lived, played and worked together in Windermere. Under the policy of separate development Windermere was erased by the apartheid state between 1958 and 1963. This chapter tells the story of how Windermere residents lived, how the state forcibly removed all residents classified African and white, and rebuilt a housing area for residents classified coloured.[2]

The 1920s to the 1940s: Squatting on the Margins

In the early decades of the twentieth century the Windermere–Kensington area was a mixture of brick dwellings and corrugated iron and wood shanties. There were many sandy patches, Port Jackson bushes, grass pastures and 'lakes' of rainwater during the winter months. During the 1900s to the 1930s, the area consisted of farmlands and subdivided plots, which were gradually sold and rented to white, Asian, coloured and African homeowners and squatters. At this time squatters in Windermere were mainly coloured, with a sprinkling of Africans and poor whites. These squatters tended to be rural migrants in search of a place to work and live in the urban

Family life in Windermere, 1947

(South African Library)

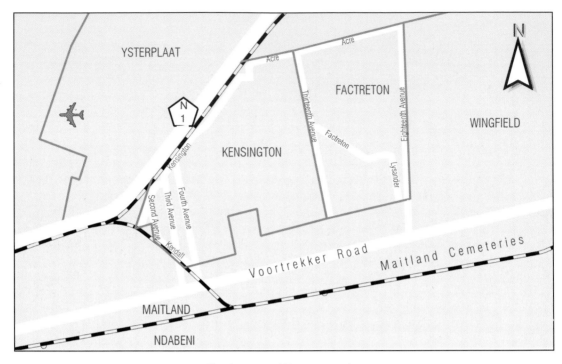

Kensington and Factreton today

areas. An African interviewee explains why he came to Cape Town in the 1930s:

> It had some attraction. Also my friend, we have been attending, him advise that Cape Town is very nice. And the money, the wages is very high in Cape Town. People will buy clothes, you get clothes very cheaper. That's why I did Cape Town. Then forever since I came to Cape Town. I study to nine. I study night school. (Mr D.R.)[3]

Windermere was attractive because of its semi-rural character, which allowed people to keep sheep, cattle, goats and other livestock. A Divisional Council census of 1923 claimed that there were roughly 2 000 people living in the area.[4] During this time, the section between 2nd and 6th Avenues was known as Kensington Estate and the neighbouring section between 6th and 13th Avenues as Kensington Estate Reserve. In 1928, the name of the area was changed to Windermere. The

new name referred to Lake Windermere in England and was chosen because of the large *vlei* (lake) that dominated the centre of the community.

Until 1943, the Cape Town municipal boundary was 6th Avenue, which included Maitland and old Kensington and excluded Windermere. The Windermere area was between 6th and 18th Avenues and fell under the control of the Divisional Council.[5] This meant that limited services were provided. It also meant that squatters could avoid paying municipal taxes and other official regulations, but still live close to their workplaces at the Cape Town docks and Wingfield airbase. During the Second World War labour shortages in the manufacturing industries and military undertakings attracted thousands of rural African workers to the cities. A coloured interviewee remembered the African influx:

> *Wat ek kan goed onthou, dat Windermere, was mieste boste gewies daai tyd, toe's daar nog nie soe baie swart mense ... Op die loop van jare hier*

A typical single-room shanty in Windermere, without sewerage, electricity or plumbing

(University of Cape Town Libraries/Manuscripts and Archives)

na die oorlog tyd in neëntien honderd neen-en-dertig, veertig, daar het die swartes begin inkom in Windermere, baie van hulle. [What I can remember well, that Windermere was mostly bushes that time, then there were not so many black people ... With the run of years, here about the war time in nineteen thirty-nine, forty, there the blacks began to come in, into Windermere, many of them.] (Mr D.S.)

The population of Windermere increased rapidly during the war years and was further stimulated by a food famine in the Transkei and Ciskei during 1945/6. The industrial strip of factories along Voortrekker Road next to Windermere–Kensington also attracted work seekers. The Medical Officer of Health (MOH) conducted a 'slum survey' (covering three-quarters of Windermere) in 1946. This survey claimed that there was a total population of 14 235 consisting of 557 European, 7 138 coloured, 6 436 African and 104 Indian residents.[6] Considering the African influx during the early 1940s the coloured majority seems questionable. Also, informal population estimates for the area vary from 20 000 to 35 000.[7]

Windermere is only fifty feet above sea level, and for most of the year vulnerable to flooding. Flooding was a source of both amusement and suffering. Several interviewees spoke of how they would wake up on winter mornings and find a layer of water over the floor.

Die wat ons nou sit, die was 'n hele rivier, daar van Voortrekker Road, daar van't af het hy deur geloop tot binne in Graaf se Bos. Dit was amper soos 'n klein seetjie gewees, mense kon nie daai tyd hier deur gekom't nie. Dit was net in somer, in winter moet jy maar Main Road om gaan. Dit was die enigste harde pad was hier 18th Avenue. Hier was 'n paar plase hier op. Boere wat hier geboer met skape, beeste en soe aan. Ja, dié was maar 'n hele wildernis gewees. [Here we now sit, this was a whole river, there from Voortrekker Road, from there down it ran to inside Graaf's Bush. It was nearly like a small sea, that time people could not come through here. It was only in summer, in winter you must go around Main Road. The only hard road was 18th Avenue. Here above were a few farms. Farmers that farmed with sheep, cattle and so on. Yes, this was a whole wilderness.] (Mr H.B.)

Windermere floods, 1948

(South African Library)

Another interviewee said:

Ooooh! We used to go in the floods. I'm telling you, the highest, you had to take your suitcase and put it onto your head. And your underwears, and you go in the dark so you can dry quickly and dress for school, near the bus stop. That time you are shivering in the train but you must go to school. My mother was very strict about school. (Mrs E.M.)

Although there was all this water most of it was undrinkable.[8] Initially two water pipes supplied water to the whole of Windermere. This water was sold at six pence a gallon. Some residents sunk their own boreholes.

It was very uncomfortable because we didn't have water. Penny a tin and carry it to the house. Toilets we didn't had. And, but later

on when we sort of got a little stake, my father built a pothollie in his place and then we sell water to the other people again. There were those times. (Mrs R.C.)

In 1937, the Windermere People's Association was formed to fight for an improvement of water, sanitation, drainage, roads and lighting.[9] The bucket system, as it was commonly known, was a widespread feature of Windermere's sanitary system.

[F]ifteen cents to bury your shit *pel*, I got customers. Sunday nights you know these guys come from Langa having a party and that fucking shit tin look like a ice cream cone. You had to pull it with a spade. But don't let me find you there tomorrow. You bury my customer's shit, we gonna fight, that's my customer. That's fifteen cents in my

pocket, one in six, whatyoucallit, it was beautiful [laughs]. (Mr G.M.)

From the 1940s, sections of the Windermere–Kensington area became dominated by thousands of corrugated iron shanties. The two main iron shanty concentrations were *Mtsheko* (derived from the word shack) and *Nommer Drie* (Number Three). *Mtsheko* was situated in the mid-section between 8th and 12th Avenues, whereas *Nommer Drie* was the section in the far corner (near the N1), roughly between 13th and 18th Avenues. A former resident and rent collector said:

You know they were clean and so forth. Shanties were lined out with jam tin labels,

Windermere floods, 1962

(South African Library)

Residents buying water from a stand pipe, ca. 1938

(South African Library)

the labels of jam tins and whatever is wherever. And you know this chap works at the printing works and this is the wastage that lines out his shanty ... Just a big scare was if a fire should break out, it destroys a lot at a time. (Mr H.V.)

Like the squatter settlements of today – for example Marconi Beam – Windermere often suffered fire damage because people used open wood fires and primus stoves. The fact that most shanties were made from wood and were built very close to each other made it easy for the fires to spread in the windy conditions of Cape Town. In 1949/50 approximately eleven fires burnt down four hundred shanties, leaving an estimated two thousand people homeless and killing three individuals.[10]

The 1940s to the 1950s: Slumyard Cultures

Windermere residents were exposed to many problems, but they were nevertheless able to create dynamic cultural relationships. Within the *Mtsheko* section, striking structures known as the 'Timberyard' and the 'Strongyard' were legendary within the local folklore of Windermere and Cape Town. The slumyards were squares of tin shanties facing inward, towards an open area. There were usually only one or two entrances into this yard of shanties. In the open area people hung up washing, children played, and people sold meat, vegetables and *umqombuti* (African beer). The yards were infamous for their concentration of illegal shebeens.

Ooooh, Mtsheko, was hier naby, wat SHAWCO nou is, daai was Mtsheko gewies.[11] Daar was net Bantoes, die Bantoes en kleurlinge het mos saam gebly ... dit was een ry pondokkies gewies. Soos die pondok huisies, dan bly 'n kleurling hier, hier bly 'n Bantoe, rye, rye huise ... dit was mense en

After the 1957 fire

(South African Library)

People living on the streets after the 1957 fire

(South African Library)

hoenders en diere het almal in een kraal gewies. Jy kan sê, die mense het gebly saam met die diere same, dit was nou Timberyard gewies, dit was Strongyard gewies. [Mtsheko was nearby where SHAWCO is now, there was Mtsheko. There were just Bantus, of course the Bantus and coloureds lived together ... it was one row of shanties. As the shanties, then a coloured lives here, and here lives a Bantu, rows, rows of houses ... it was people and chickens and animals in one kraal. You could say the people lived with the animals, this was now Timberyard, this was Strongyard.] (Mrs C.S.)

Interviewees claim that some of these yards consisted of as many as a hundred or more shanties. For many African women, selling meat, vegetables and African beer was a major source of income. While some focused on making and selling home-brewed beer, others expanded their operations into household shebeen businesses. By the mid-1940s, there were an estimated '700 to 900 shebeens at Windermere'.[12] Mrs A.D. describes how to make *umqombuti*:

You, you buy *mtombo* [sorghum], and you buy *mielie* [maize] meal. You boil your water, you put in *mielie* meal in a pail. When the water comes to boil you take cold water so the water mustn't be too hot, must be luke-warm water. Then you pour your *mielie* meal ... then you leave it, must stay overnight. Then you cook it outside, make fire ... you take those other four packets there. You put it, it's like pap now. Porridge, it's like porridge, you take those *mtombos* and you pour it in there. Then you take say, a big spoon, then you stir it. Then you take something and cover it. The next day you strain it. Ah, it's our custom, our custom. (Mrs A.D.)

The police regularly raided the yards and houses. '[T]hey make a lot at *Mtsheko*. So when the

men come, they sell it to the people. But when police come, and the drums standing there, they kick the drums, all a waste of time, waste of money. They used to come every weekend' (Mrs M.N.). Police crackdowns aimed to protect the selling of beer through legal premises. In terms of the Liquor Act of 1928 and Natives (Urban Areas) Act of 1945, 'no one anywhere in the Union may sell, supply or deliver any liquor to an African'.[13] These laws resulted in many coloured men being employed either by shebeen keepers (mainly African women) or by individual African men and women to buy alcohol for their own personal use. These liquor-running coloured men (known as mailers) mainly bought wine, brandy and other spirits.

We would go and buy liquor for them. And what we did, we would come first and open the, the, those bottles, we'd pour out a quarter of brandy out of every bottle. If we had four bottles, we'd pour out quarters then we had a bottle for ourselves ... We'd fill it up

View from Windermere looking towards Table Mountain from the SHAWCO building

(University of Cape Town Libraries/Manuscripts and Archives)

Mr C.B.

Mr C.B. was born in 1916 in Middledrift, Transkei. As a young child he worked as an animal herder. After reaching Standard Six (Grade Eight) he went with the 'big boys' to work on the gold mines of Johannesburg. From 1934 to 1943 he moved to and fro between his birthplace and the gold mines of Johannesburg. In 1943 he decided, 'I'm tired to work that side now, I must change, come to Cape Town.' On arrival in Cape Town he moved directly into Windermere.

In Cape Town he had a series of jobs ranging from hospital cleaner to security guard. Mr C.B. was pessimistic about the future. But when talking about his recreational and illegal activities in Kensington there were sparks of enthusiasm. 'Sit like this! Buy kaffir beer and drink. And even in Kensington we stay in street like this. Buy the kaffir beer and sit in the sun, whole day and drink.' Mr C.B. increased his income through the illegal selling of alcohol, *dagga*, and stolen red meat. He would steal cows from the local white farmers, which he then slaughtered and concealed: 'If I buy one this week, I'm got a receipt. Next week I'm go to steal it. I show with that receipt ... When *mabhulu* [police] he came, he saw de meat, show the receipt, there's my receipt to dem.'

At the end of the interview he said, 'I was rich man, there was rich, *maar* [but] it was not rich. Ah! 'Cos when you came here I was a man of the men. They were men of the men.' In Kensington (in the years before forced removals) he had become a successful trader with relative wealth and status. Removal to Guguletu destroyed his opportunities for illegal trading and as he suggests it also threatened his masculinity and sense of self-worth. In the interview he grasped the chance to tell heroic stories about a time when he was one of the 'men of the men'.

with water, and take six, no, seven sticks of nitrogen, matchsticks light it, put it inside, take it out and screw ... to re-charge it. To re-charge it, give its potency [laughs wickedly]. We re-charge honestly and we would shake it up, and wait for it to settle, then we had these little particles floating on top. We'd remove all that, close the bottle, turn it upside down. Take the back of a spoon, like this, and seal the bottle. They were none the wiser. But then afterwards they discovered we were crooking them. (Mr A.W.)

In contrast, an African customer describes his experience of dealing with coloured mailers:

That time you never allowed to, we used to send the *skollies* [hooligans]. Eh, eh coloured *skollie*, then pay him. Hmm ha! Doesn't matter whether you are a decent somebody, driving a good car, wearing a suit but if you are black you cannot go to, you are not allowed to buy beer, you are not allowed to have a bottle. They used to search us, *né*

[yes], they used to have to search us. If they'll find even, if you have a glass, they found a glass in your hand they going to take you. Be arrested, under arrest, for being in possession of liquor. (Mr A.Z.)

During the 1940s, Windermere was also well known for its music and dance halls. These halls were often people's homes. Many interviewees spoke of dancing to township jazz. 'We used to love dance there. Sing and dance there. We don't go home ... Seventh Avenue had lots of parties there you know? Parties, dance and pianos ... Hey! *Jika* [jive] man!' (Mr D.Y.). He also recalls dancing at the old Methodist Church, where 'admission was ten cents' and every time 'if you want to dance you pay again'. And only 'two pairs' were allowed 'on the stage' at any time. This was also the time in which Dollar Brand (now known as Abdullah Ibrahim) played as a young, unknown jazz pianist. Mr L.S. played in a dance band: 'I played the violin ... I played guitar too and a little bit of sax ... The Kensington Dance Band that's what they call it. It was mostly grown-up men and I was the only youngster' (Mr L.S.).

Shebeens ranged from the informal household business to the more developed trading of liquor and *dagga* (cannabis) by local street gang formations. Gangs with names like the Black Diamonds (between 6th and 10th Avenues), the Elephant Kids and the Peanut Boys (around Third Avenue) controlled different streets and avenues of Windermere–Kensington.

> *Nou die Elephant Kids en die Peanut Boys hulle was meer pickpocketers, gentlemen, ons was vuilgatte gewees. Black Diamonds was meer ghettoes gewees ... Kyk die bioscope was die draw card gewees, Rio bioscope, almal moet mekaar daar kry en dit is waar die [hits his hands] die bakleiry aangegaan't.* [Now the Elephant Kids

Mother and child outside a shack, 1964

(South African Library)

and the Peanut Boys they were more pickpocketers, gentlemen, we were the dirty bums. Black Diamonds were more the ghettoes ... Look the bioscope was the draw card, Rio bioscope, everyone meets there and that is where the fighting went on.] (Mr G.M.)

Sections inside the Rio bioscope were marked out according to gang formations, whereas other sections were for families and children. American movies, especially gangster and cowboy westerns, were particularly popular with gang members and youngsters in the community. But there are many stories filled with violence and sadness. 'Actually one night, a couple of guys attacked him, he was so strong, he conquer all of them and he became the leader of the Black Diamond Legion ... We were in Windermere, Seventh Avenue, bottom of Seventh Avenue, that is where they killed my brother, brutally murdered him' (Mr G.M.).

The appeal of Windermere was partly due to its being on the outside of municipal controls. But police and government officials repeatedly invaded the community. These invasions into Windermere were connected to the more powerful white community, and its fears about this expanding black community. A 'jockey' explains how her business at Windermere's 'horse racing track' was prevented:

> *Die polisie het altyd aangehou, aangehou, aangehou. Die mense het soe gepraat daarvan. En betykeer complain hulle ook van ou Hannah, het baie geld gekry en als soe, en bety kom nou en complain ... Van die perde besigheid en elke week het die plek te bietjie, te verspoelig, te aangegaan. Toe stop die polisie dit.* [The police came all the time, on and on and on. The people talked so much about it. And sometimes they also complain, about old Hannah who got so much money and some complain ... From the horse business every week, the place was a bit, too awash to go on. So the police stopped it.] (Mr H.M.)

The cultural activities of Windermere helped residents to survive the harsh economic and

Sub-economic housing scheme, Factreton, 1964

(South African Library)

political circumstances of the area financially and emotionally. These activities were like creative webs that made daily life more meaningful and at times more enjoyable.

The 1940s to the 1960s: Removals and Relocations

Before 1943 the removal of people was delayed by the lack of resources and political will of the Divisional Council. Removals that did occur were executed under the Slums Act of 1934. This Act prohibited the overcrowding and inhabiting of unhealthy dwellings. Slums Act removals targeted the African residents of Windermere, who were relocated to Langa. However, housing in Langa was already full by 1938. Before 1937 Africans were allowed to purchase land and property in Cape Town, but the Natives (Urban Areas) Amendment Act of 1937 made this very difficult.[14] By the late 1930s the lack of housing for Africans in the Western Cape had become a social and political crisis.

The Native Affairs Department stepped up its use of influx control measures under the Native Urban Areas Acts, which were used to remove African men and some African women to Langa. The term 'bachelor' loosely applied to any African male who was not married under statutory law. By 1958, over 12 000 so-called bachelors had been moved from Windermere to Langa.[15] Because of overcrowded conditions in both Windermere and Langa, plans for developing Nyanga into 'a model

Family life in Kensington

(South African Library)

Midwife and nursing assistant, Windermere, 1950

(South African Library)

Native metropolis' were announced.[16] But this was slowed down by inter-governmental arguments over the cost of housing, and legal difficulties in removing squatters from settlements like Windermere and Blouvlei (in Retreat).

From the late 1940s the Cape Town City Council developed the new coloured township of Factreton, which was situated between 13th and 18th Avenues.[17] But plans for coloured housing in Factreton could proceed only if sufficient iron shanties were demolished in the main *Mtsheko*

section of Windermere. While most of Windermere's coloured squatters were moved into new homes in Factreton, others were removed to other housing areas like Grassy Park. There were several incidents in which coloured and African squatters were left out in the winter cold after their shacks had been demolished.[18]

The first major pass raid in Windermere took place in 1948; thereafter these were frequent, especially in the period after 1953. This was because the apartheid state had refined and consolidated its pass laws in 1953. Every African interviewee complained of his or her 'bad times' under 'the pass'. Mrs M.N. shouted, 'Phew, it was terrible! It was terrible that time with passes. Oh! Everywhere you walk you've got to have your pass on your pocket ... Lot of people going to jail when they haven't got a pass on them.' And Mrs A.G. said:

Oh! A lot of bad things. We struggle with the pass, you know. The pass come 1953, I think. First they give the papers, pink papers. If you not ten years here in Cape Town, you under employment in one place, you not qualified here, you must go, with the husband, home. The people struggled very hard with the pass. The police come with the van, and uh, got dogs in the van. Fighting with the people with the dogs. And when the pass starts, you can't go to the shop. When the police stop you and 'where's your pass?' 'No my pass is in my house.' They take you, put you in the van. You must go and pay. But you've got a pass. (Mrs A.G.)

Windermere residents resisted these raids. Concerned about press reports condemning their early morning pass raids into Windermere, one senior Native Affairs Department official sent the following correspondence to another:

Past experience has shown that inspections at Windermere during the night (say between 9.00 p.m. and midnight) are extremely dangerous – the area is not well lighted and once the undesirable element (both native and coloured) realise that officials are operating in the area, stones, bottles, etc. are thrown from all angles in the dark – you will recall that on similar operations some years ago, my own car was severely damaged and had to be towed away. If these operations are carried out just before dawn, one is able to at least see where the bricks are coming from and take evasive action, but due to the fact that it is practically light this seldom happens ...[19]

By the mid-1950s many of these raids were used to hasten the process of removing 'bachelors' from Windermere to Langa. In one such raid 'more than 4 000 natives were screened when the police swooped on Windermere at 5 a.m.'.[20] By late 1957, when most of the 'bachelors' had been removed to Langa, the procedure of dealing with African families began.

Mrs C.S.

Mrs C.S. was born in Swellendam in 1922. After growing up on several farms she moved to Windermere in 1950. While unable to read or write, she said at one point, 'dan is ek slim deur my gedagte' [then I am clever through my thoughts]. She also spoke of her love for ballroom and jive dancing, which is how she met her African husband, who was a drummer in a band. They lived in Timberyard. Mrs C.S.'s family was nearly removed together with other mixed married couples. This was averted by her husband's death in 1962. 'Ek het swaar dae gehad na my man se gesterwe. Want ek was Ma. Ek was Pa. Ek was alles toe gewies.' [I had heavy days after my husband's death. Because I was mother. I was father. I was everything then.] She was a textile worker for seven years, but was retrenched when she contracted an asthmatic reaction to textile fibres. After that she worked as a domestic worker for several white families until she retired.

Although she now lives in a sub-economic brick house, she said: 'Ek sê maar elke dag, as ek nou 'n zinc huis kry in Windermere, wat daar nou zinc huise gewies't, dan het ek soentoe getrek, na my ou dorp toe. Dit was baie lekker daar gewies. Dit was mis vloer huise gewies, nie soes die huise nie, ons moet maar mis gaan haal't, dan moet onse huise gesmeer. Ons plak pampiere in die zinc huise. Ek maak dit mooi. Jy kan vuur gemaak't as dit koud is ... soos Sun City is daai plek.' [I say every day, if I can now get a zinc house in Windermere, as there were zinc houses then, then I would move to my old village. It was very nice there. It was dung floor houses, not like houses today. We used to fetch our dung and we had to smear our houses. We plastered papers in the zinc houses. It was pretty. You could make a fire when it is cold ... like Sun City was that place.]

I say, 'No if haven't got a house for me, I'm not built a *pondokkie* [shack] again, never.' So now I fight, he doesn't want to give ... I come to Langa. Umm to Mr Rogers, I say, 'Mr Rogers I not prepared to move to go and stay in the *hokkies* [transit camp dwellings], if there is no house for me just leave me here, in the Windermere.' And then I said to him, 'You give us the pass, you said the pass, we've got a right if you've ten years here and fifteen years when you are employed you know. So I'm not coming yesterday to Cape Town, I'm growing up here. ... You move out from house and then you say I must go to the *pondokkie, hayi kona* [no].' And then they leave me ... (Mrs A.G.)

Individuals like Mrs A.G., who had permanent residence rights, eventually had to move to Guguletu. In 1956 a transit camp was established at Nyanga West for African families from Windermere, Blouvlei and other squatter settlements in the Cape.[21] African individuals were legally split into three categories: those who 'qualified' for permanent residence in Cape Town; those who were 'illegals' and had a link to rural areas; and those who were 'displaced' and allocated temporary accommodation until place could be found for them in the rural areas. Thousands of African families were literally torn apart by these laws. The narrow legal definitions of a 'family' imposed by the Native Affairs Department meant that thousands of African families were split up when so-called bachelors were removed. Many African men had coloured wives.

Dit het 'n groot impact gehad oor die swartes, selfs 'n sekere deelte van die kleurlinge. Dit het ook baie kleurling vroue van hulle manne af geneem, want baie van hulle het swart mans gehad. Met die implementering van hierdie Groep Area, toe kan hulle nie saam met die mans nie. Toe moes hulle agter bly met die kinders, en dit is waarom jy sal vind in die area, nog steeds dat kinders is gebaster, kinders is gemeng, want die vader was

---

Mrs F.M.

Mrs F.M. was born in 1910 in Idutywa, Transkei. She left her birthplace in 1934 and moved to inner-city Buitenkant Street, Cape Town. She moved to Windermere in 1949. Between 1960 and 1969 she had various 'sleep-in' jobs as a domestic worker for white families in Cape Town. From 1969 to 1976 she lived in Guguletu. From 1976 she lived in Nyanga old-age home until she died in 1996.

Mrs F.M. had a strong interest in the law. She said, 'If I was a boy, I would turn out to be a policeman [laughs]. In those times there was no policewomen.' Her interest in legal issues began with her policeman father. In contrast, her memories of Windermere are filled with depressing images of it being 'crowded' with people and lots of 'pigs, dams and dirty water'. She lived at Number 51 Timberyard. She spoke of how she was 'miserable then' from living in *pondokkies* and working long hours as a domestic worker.

She did not like Windermere because 'most of our people were tribal, you know, and if you don't be drinking and doing that, it's not nice ... then they start to fight with sticks and then stabbing too, you know, that's why I don't like drinking, they will fight over this drink no'. She developed a strong sense of morality through her involvement in the Catholic Church. Mrs F.M. believed that 'a person is just like another person, you cut from this one, blood comes, you cut from this one, blood comes, you see everybody is in the image of God. To say it's white, it's black is nothing, that's why I don't like apartheid'. Her belief in a common 'blood' beneath the different skin colours of people is a story told by many interviewees. It is a belief that beyond the oppression and divisions of apartheid all people are really human.[22] She expressed her gratitude by commenting, 'I must say myself, to say out and listen to people, and be friendly with people that's very nice, it's a cure for me to and do pray for me, I'll pray for you.'

weggeneem, omdat hy swart is. Dit was meeste onder die bruin vroue, wat die lyding moes deurgaan het, die Groep Areas Act. [It had a big impact on the blacks, even on a portion of the coloureds. It also removed many coloured women from their husbands because they had taken black husbands. With the implementation of the Group Area, they could not go with the men. They remained behind with the children and that is why you will still find many illegitimate children, children of mixed descent, as the father was taken away, because he was black. It was mainly the coloured women who experienced suffering, the Group Areas Act.] (Mr D.S.)

While pass laws were aimed at people classified African, the Group Areas Act was aimed at everyone. In 1958 the Land Tenure Advisory Board zoned Windermere–Kensington as a 'coloured area'. In the same year, white families were told to

Officials visiting Windermere in 1962

(South African Library)

leave the area. A white interviewee describes his memory of the day his family had to leave:

> I will never forget that day, that we had to move. My mother cried like a baby, also my father because of the big grounds, we enjoyed life there. My father liked gardening and we made extra money selling vegetables and, and flowers to the coloured people. Like I said, it was terrible, it was not a nice scene to see, the day we, when we moved because we loved that place, especially my mother. (Mr D.K.)

The Land Tenure Advisory Board claimed that there were '842 Europeans' living in the area who would have to move.[23] By contrast, there were still '2 800 Native families living in Windermere (a

SHAWCO students with children, 1969

(University of Cape Town Libraries/Manuscripts and Archives)

Children who are part of a SHAWCO childcare programme drinking cooldrink, Windermere, 1969

(University of Cape Town Libraries/Manuscripts and Archives)

total population of 13 000) who cannot be moved until accommodation has been provided at Nyanga West'.[24] When African interviewees spoke about these events, a mixture of feelings surfaced:

We, we shhew! Some of the people cried too, they didn't want to come here, but what could you do? Got to go out, and they warn you, 'Go out, go there!' The following day they break the *pondokkies* down ... Oh 'twas terrible, some people come here in the night with the lorry with the clothes in. (Mrs M.N.)

I don't know why we did move. We ask mother why we were moving there, because that place nice and quiet and we used to stay with the coloured people. So my mother say, 'No we must move' ... It was only the Africans who moved out, only the coloureds stays there, because even now it's only coloureds there, there's no Africans. (Mrs A.D.)

As a coloured observer of these events put it, 'I've seen at that time, I couldn't see more crueller people than those Bantu inspectors. Nothing arranged. Just force. Just force' (Mr K.N.). In the Nyanga West transit camp Africans were placed in temporary houses. Some people remained there for three to four years. Permanent housing eventually became available in Section 2, Nyanga, which was renamed Guguletu in 1962. By 1963 there were only '30 Native families left in Windermere'.[25] According to informants the last of the African families to be removed from Windermere tended to be property owners who received little compensation.

Resistance to these removals was fragmented by the brute force of the state and the making of false promises (i.e. move to 'nice new houses' in Guguletu). 'What can I do, it's the law, it's the law,

Mr D.K.

Mr D.K. was born in 1937, into a family of eighteen children (plus one adopted child) in Windermere. He grew up as a white child amongst African and coloured friends and neighbours. His family was removed from Windermere to the neighbouring white suburb of Maitland in 1958. When asked why his family originally moved into Windermere, he replied, '... because of the size of the house, the size of the ground, it was open life, it, it was beautiful there. It was like living on a farm.' His father was a bus driver and his mother was a housewife. He also recalled the following memory from the 1950s: 'Coloureds upstairs and whites downstairs, and his standing at the bus stop, you talk, you laugh and the bus arrives now you must go downstairs and he must go upstairs that was a terrible thing.'

Today, Mr D.K. is a distribution manager for a major food company and also a member of the old Apostolic Church. While he now lives in a middle-class white suburb, like most interviewees, he misses his youthful days in the old area. 'Those years, like I said, coloured people were beautiful to us and we were beautiful to them, there were no problems between us. And they used to call us on our name and we used to call them on their name. There was no hatred, there wasn't a thing called politics. No apartheid there. Although there was signs but for us that area, there was no apartheid because we were friends. We were united in those years and we never had problems. We were great friends.'

what can I do – nothing. It was not nice leaving those people, you see, I was so ... I was not happy. I didn't know this place, how this place is' (Mrs E.P.). Another African interviewee said:

[E]k was nou nie kwaad, ons was mos bang vir die gowerment. Ons moet huis uit gaan. Wat hulle sê dat hulle het vir ons huise gebou, toe't ons kom in die huise in gaan. [I wasn't angry, we were scared of the government. We must get out of the house. What they say, that they have built houses for us, so we went into the houses.] (Mrs P.G.)

The children of this generation of Windermere residents later fought political struggles against the apartheid state and engaged in the school boycotts of 1976, 1980 and 1985 in Cape Town. This generation of students, residents and workers from both African and coloured 'group areas' united to build anti-apartheid organisations such as the United Democratic Front, the Western Cape Youth League and the Unity Movement in the 1980s.

Looking back at the first half of this century, squatters, tenants and homeowners came into Windermere in search of a secure place to build a home and a community. Windermere desperately

needed major social and economic development. While the apartheid state promised social uplift-ment, it in fact used racist legislation and forced removals to destroy the Windermere community. By the mid-1960s all African, white and Asian residents, as well as some coloured residents, had been removed from the area.[26]

Where Windermere once stood, middle-class Kensington (from 2nd to 13th Avenues) and the working-class housing estate of Factreton (between 13th and 18th Avenues) can be found today. But the Windermere story does not end here. The thousands who were moved into Factreton, Langa and Guguletu and to the so-called homelands of the Transkei and Ciskei took with them their memories of Windermere. In Guguletu there is a Kensington Burial Society that still meets on a regular basis. And in Kensington itself there are schools named Windermere Primary and Windermere High. These are all reminders of the Windermere past, before forced removals. For some, these memories might have little meaning. For most people, especially those that still refer to themselves as 'Windermere people', these memories are a way of holding onto the meaningful actions, people and events of their lives.

4 'Everyone had their differences but there was always comradeship': Tramway Road, Sea Point, 1920s to 1961[1]

Michele Paulse

This chapter presents a brief look at aspects of life in the Sea Point neighbourhoods of Tramway Road and Ilford Street before the forced removals of the late 1950s and early 1960s. Situated on the hills below Lion's Head, Tramway Road stretched between the busy main roads of Regent Road and Kloof Road, with Ilford Street branching directly off Tramway Road. Although a culturally mixed area, this community was largely made up of coloured working-class families. It was part of the larger middle-class white suburb of Sea Point that formed part of Cape Town's Atlantic seaboard. The residents of Tramway Road lived in a small and contained suburban pocket. Extended family and neighbourhood networks, established over generations, provided a strong sense of identity and community spirit that cut across social boundaries.

A northern view of Tramway Road with the (whites-only) King's Road Primary School behind the trees, 1960

(District Six Museum)

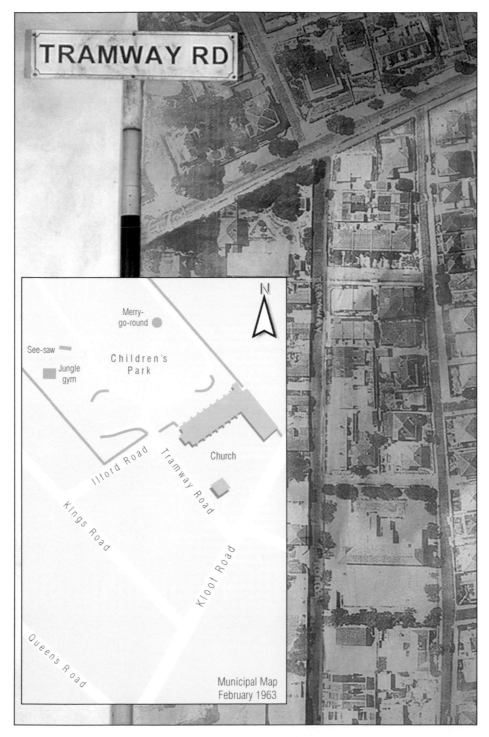

This wall exhibit in the District Six Museum shows the suburban pocket of Tramway Road and Ilford Street

(District Six Museum)

Today, the communities of Tramway Road and Ilford Street no longer exist. A fenced, locked park with a gate now blankets the middle of Tramway Road and divides it into two parts: Tramway Road at the lower end and Ilford Street at the upper end, which intersects with Kloof Road. These oral history interviews with ex-Tramway Road and Ilford Street residents explore the implications of living in a suburban pocket. The interviews trace the ways in which economic, social and political circumstances moulded these communities and demonstrate the devastating effects of forced removals.

Life in a Suburban Pocket

Many Tramway Road residents trace their families' origins back to the late nineteenth century. The mid-area of Tramway Road became a residential site in 1877 when the Cape Town and Green Point Tramway Company built cottages for its employees, white tram guards and coloured tram drivers, grooms and stablemen. In 1895 the Tramway Company closed and gradually other residents moved into the area. By 1903, twenty-five cottages, fourteen houses and a small block of flats stood where the park is now situated. From the 1920s, mainly coloured families and smaller numbers of Africans, Indians and whites lived in the mid-area. Coloured, Indian and white families occupied six houses in Ilford Street.

Custom in the Cape Colony before 1910 and later laws after Union in South Africa restricted the majority of people of colour to the working class.[2] Work

formed one of the main reasons for residence in Tramway Road and Ilford Street, as many residents worked in the homes and businesses of white Sea Point families. Several of the men worked as painters, carpenters, drivers, delivery men and cooks. Men also worked for the municipality of Green Point and Sea Point, and, after merging in 1913, for the City of Cape Town. The majority of the women worked as washerwomen and domestic workers. Mrs C.T., who lived in the Council flats and had moved to Tramway Road in 1935 at the age of 15, said, 'My mother got married … my father was working in the Council … he was a rate weigher [refuse collector]. That time it was horses and carts. No lorries or buses for the dirt, you know? … That's why. He was working at the Council.'

In 1961, of forty-four families in Tramway Road and Ilford Street, thirteen families earned under R40 per month, twenty-seven between R40 and R140 and four families earned more than R140.[3] Low wages and the cost of living affected the chances of Tramway Road and Ilford

Men of Tramway Road. From left to right: Esau Phillips, John Mitchell and Melvin Mitchell in Bellevue Road, Sea Point, 1956

(District Six Museum)

Violet Peterson standing in her yard at
7 Tramway Road, 1960

(District Six Museum)

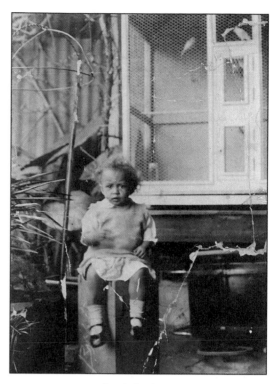

Beattie Jacobs at
4 Tramway Road

(District Six Museum)

Street residents. Children usually left school from the age of 12 to work and contribute a wage to the household income. Ex-Ilford Street resident Mrs A.D., born in 1915, recollected that household finances shortened her years of education:

> So you see, our, my children by then could get a chance to go after their schooling. They could move out of, go and do a job hairdressing or factory or whatever – secretary – we could afford. But we, like my lot, couldn't get a chance. There was no money. There was no chance for us to get a good schooling.

The Parker and Tiseker families owned their own homes, but most residents rented their homes, as they could not afford to buy property. The majority of the residents were subtenants or had a subtenant. A shortage of housing and high rents meant that two and sometimes three households lived in one house. Mrs P.G., who was born in 1927 and moved with her brother and widowed father from a house in Tramway Road to District Six in 1937, recalled where she stayed in Tramway Road:

> We stayed three families. In the first we had three bedrooms. One room we stayed, the room the Colsons stayed, one room the Arendses stayed. Everybody was staying with people. Look that time it was the money was nothing and there was not how we didn't, nobody had a house. You follow? Nobody as old as I know had a house in Tramway Road. The only people that [had] a property was the shop and I think the shoemaker. But we all stayed in rented houses.

The Parker family

(District Six Museum)

To accommodate each other, members of a household had to organise their lives to permit space to everyone. Males and females of different ages who lived in the same room devised strategies for privacy. Space being a problem, members of the same household did many activities together. Mrs G.E., born in 1932, recalled the conditions in her parental household:

> Everybody was happy. That time we never even thought about 'we too cramped out. We must move out'. We were so happy with each other that we just stayed close. Everybody was very, very, very close to their family. That is how they grew up. That is how we grew up. Very, very close to that is why when we meet each other we are still like that. A close-knitted family. The entire road was a close-knitted family. If you needed something you'd come to my mother. My mother would give it to you. Even if it's a piece of bread.

Many residents felt a deep sense of belonging to Sea Point. This came partly from the fact that some of the households had lived in the area for generations. Well-known Tramway Road families who lived in the neighbourhood in the late 1800s and early 1900s included the Lawrence (1898), Paulsen (1900), Wepener (1901), Parker (1903) and Tiseker families (1903, if not earlier). The Jacobs family (1923) moved to Ilford Street from King's Road. Jacobus Weppenaar, a tram driver, lived in Sea Point in 1883, but it is unknown whether he was an ancestor of the Wepener household of 1901.[4] Several households were related to each other. From the 1920s to the 1950s, blood and marriage related close to twenty-six families in Tramway Road and Ilford Street. In 1959 approximately two hundred people[5] or fifty families[6] lived there. Mr R.P. spoke of his relations in Tramway Road in the late 1950s: '[My] cousins. They were down in number three. The last row of cottages at the bottom, number three. Related through my grandfather. We had the Paulsens number twenty-one, the Paulsens number seventeen, the Paulsens number three.'

Extended family helped out when people needed a loan or assistance with a job. Women went to a friend or relative to borrow items such as sugar and rice. According to Mrs A.D. of Ilford Street, financial assistance was always available during critical times.

> Yes, yes. You know you short, you got no money or something that you got little accounts you can go to one another and you know and two or three will [claps hands twice] come together and, 'here you are. Here

Identity card of ex-Tramway Road resident
M. Paulsen. The letter K indicates racial classification, i.e.
'Kleurling' (Coloured)

(District Six Museum)

you are. Go on, settle with them'.
And you would just see that you
give it back. It's not told to you, 'see
that you give it back'. But you make you
your, you make it so that you give it back
and you can go next time.

Small and often irregular household incomes
encouraged women to adopt careful financial and
shopping skills. By purchasing the least expensive
grocery items, households lived within their
means. But on Sundays, children could expect a

Mrs C.T.

Every second weekend, Mrs C.T. travels from
Hout Bay on the Atlantic Coast to her home in
Bridgetown on the Cape Flats. On Monday morning she returns to Hout Bay to the family for
whom she has worked for the past thirty years.
She moved to Silvertown in 1956 after households were forced to vacate the Council flats in
Tramway Road. She moved to Bridgetown in
1980. Born in Genadendal in 1915, Mrs C.T.
moved to the flats in Tramway Road with her
mother and father when she was 15 years old.
Her mother took in washing and worked as a
domestic worker in Sea Point. Mrs C.T. got her
first job outside of the home at the Seacliff Hotel,
at the age of 23: 'I didn't do other jobs [before
then]. We used to do washing. My mother used to
do some washing at the hotel where I worked. I
used to go and collect the washing there and then
they asked me. I started in the kitchen, washing
up the dishes and in a year's time I trained myself
up because going inside laying the table and I

trained myself like that and then they took me
from the kitchen and put me into the dining
room for the head waitress.'

Mrs C.T. stopped working 'when I got married' at the age of 25. 'Then I was just home, doing
my own home now with Ursie. I had to see to her
... Then I got another job, again. Well that was
just charring.' During her twenties she enjoyed
dancing and attended dances in Cape Town and
the suburbs. She met her late husband at a dance
at Valkenberg Hospital in Observatory. Mrs C.T.,
her husband and their daughter lived with her
widowed mother and later moved into their own
flat in the Council building. After more than thirty
years of residency on the Cape Flats, Mrs C.T. con-
siders it home. Tramway Road, she says, is part of
the past. 'No, my dear. I don't see why we should
fight for Tramway Road again. Why? Tell me. I
wouldn't fight for it. I wouldn't try to go back
again. Because it means I got to go build again ...
Do you think it's right for me to stand with them?'

special lunch and eagerly compared menus with playmates. Parents had to skimp on food expenses during the week to provide a more substantial meal on Sundays. In Christian households the afternoon meal on Sunday reflected the religious significance of the day. Ms M.M., born in 1943, recalled an inexpensive food she often ate:

> We got so sick and tired of eating that *mielie* [maize] rice. On Sunday they have this nice rice and the children ask you, 'What are you going to eat today? No, my mommy's going to make roast chicken and real rice. Not *mielie* rice, real rice and roast potatoes and we're going to have pumpkin and peas.' 'And what you going to have for pudding?' 'We going to have *lekker* [nice] red jelly and custard.' That was one of the wonderful things ... [Monday to Friday] it will be *bredies* [stew]. Saturday we would eat a sandwich ... there was once my mommy didn't have meat in the house in Sea Point. My daddy said she must try and get some tomatoes and onions and boil some rice. She boiled the rice and got the bruised tomatoes and onions ... Here we all sitting and waiting. 'When are we going to eat?' It was a cold night. Here my father came with this big parcel ... It was that penny polony.

Residents of this suburban pocket supported each other in their struggle for material survival. This shared struggle and sense of community and family was reinforced by living in an isolated pocket surrounded by white communities.

Social Boundaries and Boundary Crossings

To survive the social and political conditions of the colonial, segregation and apartheid years, residents of Tramway Road had to cross social boundaries within their community. The conditions pushed residents into low-wage occupations, which limited their life choices. Class and racial attitudes relating to differences in status and wealth also affected residential patterns in Tramway Road.

Whites lived in the mid-area of Tramway Road in the early part of the twentieth century, but the majority left in the 1930s and 1940s. In the 1950s, middle-class whites, and perhaps their live-in domestic worker, lived at the top and bottom ends of the road.

> Who wanted to come up Tramway Road? Hardly anybody. It was mostly people that lived there that would drive there. There were whites who lived in Tramway Road right at the bottom. There were three houses and right at the top there were also white people living there ... The ones right at the bottom were near the main road. The ones at the top were near to Kloof Road. And there was Seaview Terrace. They used to go down King's Road. (Mrs P.v.d.W.)

Nurses of St John's First Aid, ca. 1960. Front row: Sarah Panday, Shirley Jacobs. Back row: Sylvia Thomas, Thelma Paulsen, Ellen Davids.

(District Six Museum)

In South Africa, the separation of classes and races dated back to the colonial era. Terms such as madam and master were common during the days of slavery and were legally entrenched in the Masters and Servants Act of 1873. These terms were still in use in Cape Town and Sea Point in the 1940s and 1950s and determined how persons of colour addressed whites.[7] An ex-Tramway Road resident who was born in 1943 recollected how adults taught children the rules of a segregated society: 'We used to call them [the white people] madam and master. We were brought up that way. My mommy was working for the madam. My mommy used to tell me, "Go to madam so and so and tell her yes, I won't be in." So we got into that. It's madam and master' (Ms M.M.).

St Louis Christmas Choir, 1956

(District Six Museum)

Keith van der Westhuizen in front of John Petersen's green grocer lorry, 1960

(District Six Museum)

Although conflicting with the religious principles upheld by the Anglican Church of the Holy Redeemer, built in Tramway Road in 1922, racial preference towards white parishioners was common. 'When they [whites] come to church it's Mrs Jones or Mrs Brown' (Ms M.M.). Whites sat at the front of the church and coloureds at the back. The irony of this discrimination was not lost on the coloured members of the congregation.

Tramway Road and Ilford Street residents created distinctions among themselves and in this way expressed a characteristic found among people of all classes.[8] Social and political conditions impressed upon people of colour to represent themselves as 'respectable' persons. In Tramway Road and Ilford Street, the pressure of respectability combined with the human tendency to regard oneself as better than another. Ms M.I., an ex-Tramway Road resident, interpreted the behaviour of some Ilford Street residents to mean that they and their households were better than people in Tramway Road:

Because I know like I said to you some of the people that lived at the top where Ilford Street is. There where the church is. Some of those people they did not associate with us at all. Because they were supposed to be the middle class. You know the people still classed each other. That happens in all communities. (Ms M.I.)

Ex-Ilford Street resident Ms M.J. felt so strongly about her views of residents in Tramway Road that during her adult years in the 1940s and 1950s she avoided the road altogether. 'I didn't have anything to do with the people on Tramway Road … If I had to go down to the main road, I never went down Tramway Road. I walked down King's Road.'

People made distinctions between the Council flats and the cottages and houses in Tramway Road and Ilford Street. Erected as a hostel for African men in 1903, the Council flats acquired a bad reputation. Many coloureds subsequently lived in the flats, which were generally run-down and neglected. For a variety of reasons, tenants tended to be seen as people of questionable morality and unsafe company. Mr R.P. explained the following:

Mr R.P.: We, right at the bottom I think they belonged to the Council, we used to call that *duiwelhuis* [devil's house].
M.P.: Where did the name *duiwelhuis* come from?
Mr R.P.: Oh, it was weird. It was like dorms they had there. It was dark and no electricity … They had a flight of cement stairs and just went up into a room like a dorm and another one. We children were very afraid to go in there at night. Oh!
M.P.: Did adults ever use *duiwelhuis* as a warning to kids?
Mr R.P.: Yes, yes … They would tell you they would take us down there, threaten to take us down there. The mere mention of the place! [laughs]

But this did not keep all residents apart. Some people in the cottages and houses enjoyed friendships with residents of the Council flats. Females in Ilford Street chummed around with girls in Tramway Road. Mrs S.S., born in 1942, who lived in Ilford Street, regarded one of the cottages in Tramway Road as her second home: 'We were close-knitted. Even if our parents weren't home we could know the neighbours to see to us or things like that. The Jacobs, Mrs Davis, Peggy and I. I was a lot my Ursula's mommy. Lawrence. That was my second home.'

Ilford Street boys played with friends who lived in Tramway Road. When Mr A.J. of Ilford Street, born in 1935, recalled his friendship with boys on Tramway Road, he said, 'We were a nice group together.' In at least two cases, residents of Tramway Road and Ilford Street married each other.

Segregation and later apartheid affected the lives of Africans and coloureds dramatically. Some Africans who could pass for coloured and some coloureds who could pass for white crossed the race bar. The Native Reserve Locations Act of 1902 required Africans to live in a location unless they had a permit to live elsewhere. To reside outside the location without a permit, many Africans who could pass for coloured did so. The decision of an African man to cross the colour bar allowed him and his family to acquire residence in Tramway Road around 1944: 'Because he [my father] was very light in complexion. Those days you could you know, you could pass for coloured' (Ms C.K.).

This African household was not alone in crossing the colour bar. To enjoy amenities and services reserved for whites, some light-skinned coloureds in Tramway Road passed for white in the city at large. Patrons in cinemas reserved for whites watched a better category of film than the selection of movies shown in cinemas reserved for people of colour. Passing for white permitted an individual better service in shops and institutions such as the post office. A general animosity and mistrust against whites aroused suspicions in the Tramway Road community. Ms U.L, born in 1935, recalled that some residents disapproved of a neighbour who passed as a white person: 'There in Tramway Road we had … family members who were fair-skinned. They lived there but they went to white bioscopes. Mrs ..., she lived her way but she was actually ostracised by the rest of the community.'

The relationships and levels of interaction between members of Tramway Road and Ilford Street households varied.

Public Activity and Community

As a relatively small number of people of colour in a largely white suburb, Tramway Road and Ilford Street residents learned to keep to their neighbourhood. *'Jy moet nie gaan interfere daar met die wit mense ... met die wit mens se plekke nie.* [You must not go interfere with white people ... with the white people's places.] Stay where you belong' (Mr R.L.). Social pressure to stay within the physical boundaries of their neighbourhood combined with people's economic circumstances. Residents created and participated in public activities that involved members of many of the households, leading to the feeling that 'everyone was one' (Mrs P.G.).

Photographs belonging to Ms T.P. show Tramway Road and Ilford Street children amid the rocks and shrubs of Lion's Head in the 1940s and 1950s and provide a backdrop to her memories: 'Every Saturday afternoon, Sunday we go pick flowers. Saturday we take from Lion's Head right to Camps Bay. Walk through the mountain to the Glen ... that was our outing.' Another favourite outing for both children and adults was to walk down to the seafront. Residents valued the sea for its recreation and fish. 'The *harders* [mackerel] ... by boat we used to catch mackerel, *geelbek* [Cape salmon], galjoen ... Anglers go out and catch the galjoen,' said Mr R.P. He recalled that his father and brothers fished with the Arendse men who were known for their fishing skills. He also remembered one of his favourite pastimes: 'Used to make a fire on the beach with a paraffin tin or we bring it home and there around Number 25, used to make fire and boil the crayfish ... During crayfish season we used to go Saturdays, weekdays, during the week.'

From the 1930s to the 1950s, residents watched films organised by Mr N. Thomas and later his nephew, Mr R. Paulsen, on Wednesday evenings in St Andrew's Hall, at the Holy Redeemer Church. A notice posted at the shop of Mr Parker, a general dealer, announced the film of the week. Mr A. Tiseker operated a smaller shop just north of the Parker business, until the Tiseker household moved in 1954. Mr Parker operated a café after 6 p.m. This shop and the part of Tramway Road that lay directly outside the shop represented a public space where mostly men, teenagers, young adults and children congregated. In the years before Mr Tiseker moved, Mr Parker and Mr Tiseker often joined the men in a game of darts at the café. During the Second World War, men discussed the events of the war on Mr Parker's *stoep* (verandah). In 1938, Mrs M.L., then 12 years old, bought delicious sweets at the shop with a half-crown earned from polishing shoes for her mother's employer.

On the slopes of Lion's Head, 1951

(District Six Museum)

The Sea Point Swifts soccer club, 1941

(District Six Museum)

We could sit on the *stoep* with our legs hanging. You know that kind of *stoep* and we can sit and drink our cooldrink. We can eat our sweets or our cake there. It's the same as the road. If children play it looks indecent playing on the road [today] but that was our playground. We used to play one-leg in the road, we played *kennetjie*, skipping rope, cars. (Mrs M.L.)

Mr E.L., born in 1932, also remembered that Mr Parker's shop was a focus of public activity:

You come to the shop and always someone was there and you talk to them. One of the Arendses played the guitar. Paulsen played the mandolin. He'd play music at Allie's. Someone played a mouth organ and you want to play and that's how it started that you learn to play that instrument. Standing on Allie Parker's *stoep* was something. You could watch the girls.

In 1918 Tramway Road boys who kicked ball on the road outside the shops formed the Sea Point Swifts soccer team. Boys were recruited from Tramway Road and Ilford Street as well as from other parts of Cape Town. Residents who lived in the flats, houses and cottages cheered the team during Saturday afternoon matches at the Green Point Common and supported drives to raise funds.

Religion played an important role in households. In the 1940s and 1950s, children of the Parker household received religious instruction from the Imam of the mosque in Chiappini Street, Green Point. Members of the Nathoo household travelled to Mowbray to participate in services for followers of the Hindu faith. Tramway Road and Ilford Street residents who belonged to the Dutch Reformed Church attended services at the *Sendingkerk* (Mission Church) in Long Street. The majority of residents attended the Holy Redeemer Anglican Church and the Baptist Church. Built in Tramway Road in 1901, the Baptist Church held a Sunday School, which was attended by the majority of children, regardless of their Christian denomination.

Christian residents actively supported the Anglican and Baptist churches. Men maintained the buildings and grounds. Women baked and crafted items for church bazaars. Children and adults participated in voluntary associations and concerts. The Sunbeams (1920s), the Wayfarers (1930s) and from the 1930s through to the 1950s the Boy Scouts operated from the Holy Redeemer Church. Residents attended temperance meetings at the Baptist Church. Both churches held annual concerts that allowed Tramway Road and Ilford Street children to show off their talents.

Forced Removals: 1959 to 1961

In the 1950s the National Party intensified the racial separation that for decades characterised life in South Africa. The Group Areas Act of 1950 legislated separate residential areas and in 1957 the government ordered the removal of people of colour from Sea Point.[9] Tramway Road and Ilford Street lay in an area declared 'white' in the Government Gazette of 5 July 1957. Between 1959 and 1961 all persons of colour were removed from Tramway Road and Ilford Street to the Cape Flats.

Other forced relocations had previously taken place in Tramway Road. In 1903, under the Native Reserve Locations Act of 1902, the municipal council of Green Point and Sea Point removed African men who lived in the Council flats, then called workmen's quarters, to the Docks Location. At least three decades before the Group Areas Act declaration Tramway Road residents lived under the threat of eviction.

> And it took them a very long time to decide to put the coloured people out of Tramway Road. In 1927 one of the Sea Point ... families' son got married. Charley Petersen. And he came to our home in Woodstock and they said they are busy with them. They want to put the Tramway cottage people ... must move them. (Mrs D.L.)

The Group Areas Act encouraged 'strong talk' about forced removal in 1956. That year, tenants of the Council flats received notice to vacate their homes. 'Because they [the City Council] said they

The Sea Point Baptist Church Sunday School performing the 'Blue Danube'

(District Six Museum)

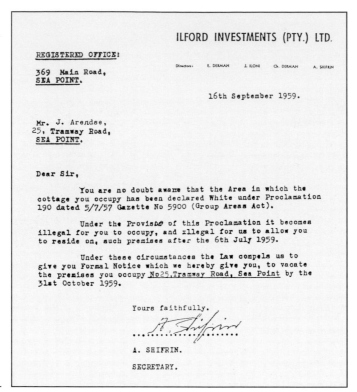

A copy of the
eviction notice Ilford
Investments sent
to Mr J. Arendse at
25 Tramway Road

(District Six Museum)

wanted that site for the council yard to be extend-ed. The yard was right next to our flats. That was the excuse. They want to extend the Council' (Mrs U.L.). The Tombeni household moved to Silvertown into a house built by the Cape Town City Council for its Council workers and their families.

Mr Ziman, landlord of houses Number 1 to 4 Tramway Road, served notice to tenants in 1957. The Shinosha family moved to town. In July 1959,

---

Mr P.J.

'Beeston', the brass name plate that hung on the gate to Mr P.J.'s house in Ilford Street, hangs on the outer front wall of his house in Bonteheuwel. Born in 1905 in King's Road, Sea Point, the street just west of Tramway Road, Mr P.J. moved to Ilford Street with his family when he was a youngster. His father was a mason brick layer, but 'I'm the only one of family dat did not want to take it up. I didn't like to work in the cement.'

Mr P.J. began his formal work life as a bottle washer in a chemist's shop. Later, he worked for the Green and Sea Point municipality. As a Council worker, he learnt to manoeuvre through the Council's bureaucracy. He also held a job at the Kings Hotel in Sea Point. After forced removal to Bonteheuwel, Mr P.J. pressed the Council to install traffic lights at an intersection and improve the walkway at the local train station.

At 93 years of age, Mr P.J. strains to hear and remember. Arthritis cripples his fingers, thick-lens spectacles aid his sight, a cane balances his walk. He notes that because of his age, 'people expect me I've got to remember. I only remember ... what I happened, what I started in my little life.' At this stage of his life, he reflects, '[a]s I sit here today as the last, eldest citizen of Sea Point ... I'm readying to go to my Lord. That is how, that is what I am preparing myself to for.' Mr P.J. died in 1999.

Tramway Road families and friends: the Lambert, Rammsami, Phillips, Mitchell and Barros families

(District Six Museum)

Tramway Road residents Daphne Barros, Katey Mitchell (with baby) and Melvin Mitchell

(District Six Museum)

a Group Areas inspector told residents that the two-year period of grace stated in the Gazette of 1957 had expired.[10] On 16 September, Ilford Investments, the owner of the cottages, sent eviction notices to tenants. They had to vacate their homes by 31 October.[11] On 18 September, Mr Nicholas Thomas and Mr John Petersen, Tramway Road residents, called on Mr Wilko Wannenburg, a lawyer and member of the Holy Redeemer congregation. 'They brought a letter that all the tenants had received ... They were alarmed, of course' (Mr W.W.).

Wannenburg advised residents to form the Tramway Road Association, which included residents of Ilford Street. He agreed to represent the Association for a nominal fee and set out to prepare an application to submit to the Group Areas Board. The Tramway Road Association declined the support of organisations that offered to protest against the neighbourhood's removal. The Association preferred to rely on their legal advice, religious faith and presentation as respectable citizens. The Association requested and received a one-year extension on residents' notice to leave their homes and received a total of three extensions.[12]

Bewildered, dismayed, fearful and confused, residents grappled to understand the notice for eviction. The notice and its implications unsettled their sense of self and dignity.[13] On Tuesday, 3 November 1959, Mr Frederick Mitchell, who raised his own family at Number 7 Tramway Road and whose elderly widowed mother lived at Number 8 Tramway Road Cottages, left his home and did not return. Mr Mitchell committed suicide and was found hanged somewhere between Camps Bay and Bakoven.[14] 'He [my father] went into something of a vacuum or ... He wasn't interested in anything ... He didn't really want to move from there. And he

Mr Ab.P. and Mr Ah.P.

Born in 1938 in Tramway Road, Mr Ab.P. is the eldest of ten children. Mr Ah.P., the second youngest, was born in 1944. The family lived at 11 Tramway Road. Both brothers and all their siblings began their education at the Tramway Road School at the Sea Point Baptist Church. When they were youngsters, the brothers worked in the shop their father owned.

Mr Ab.P.: 'We used to deliver the groceries [to people in the vicinity]. We delivered personally ... They phone the stuff, orders and then we take it to their house.'
Mr Ah.P.: 'To different places.'
Mr Ab.P.: 'They ran accounts, you know. They could buy on credit. Because the people knew each other so they pay.'

Although their mother did not work in the shop she introduced new items for sale. Mr Ah.P. said that his mother 'once came in the shop and that time afterwards she started making certain goods for the shop like coconut, iced coconut ... and *koeksisters* and things like that ... and after I remember she wanted to ... father was, was against it you know ... like people used to ... sell paraffin ... She was very adventurous in those things.' Mr Ab.P. left school at the age of 15 to work in the shop full-time because his father suffered from an injury to his eye. After Mr Ab.P. got married in February 1957, he and his wife moved into his parents' home. Today, Mr Ab.P. owns and operates a grocery shop in Mitchells Plain. Mr Ah.P. is a medical doctor in Hanover Park.

became sickly' (Mr M.M.). Mr Mitchell's suicide affected the whole neighbourhood.

> That really shook the whole community. Shook it right down to the core ... at first they still had hope. There was quite a lot of hope that we were not going to... we're going to outlive eviction. Getting a reprieve every time, staying longer and longer. But when that – okay, it became inevitable that the writing was on the wall. (Mr R.P.)

The government pressed the Cape Town City Council to develop Bonteheuwel as a township for coloureds and in 1961 Council houses became available to persons who met the criteria for sub-economic housing. Located on the Cape Flats, Bonteheuwel lay sixteen kilometres from Sea Point. Some households did not qualify for this sub-economic housing, while others rejected Bonteheuwel as a suitable option. Ms E.P., whose parents decided against the coloured township, described the traumatic events her household experienced in the six months after they left Sea Point:

> We really became a circus. We had to live here, split. The family had to split up. She [my sister] had to live in Woodstock. Myself and my [other] sister's two little girls had to go to Elsies River. My mom went to her mother. My father went to her sister, my other sister until we got this place.

With the financial help of extended family, the Nathoo household bought a house in Rylands. Part of the Parker household moved temporarily to Wynberg before buying a house in Rylands. When Mr Parker, then in his early eighties, returned to Cape Town from a visit to India in 1964, he found it difficult to adjust to Rylands. 'When my father eventually landed here he wasn't happy at all. Because he wasn't used to the place' (Mr Ab.P.).

Some residents moved to areas such as Mowbray, District Six, Lansdowne, Black River and Milnerton, only to have to move again when these areas were declared white. Individuals who travelled to Sea Point to work incurred high transportation costs. For some time after removal, women and their children continued to fetch and deliver washing in Sea Point. However, the cost of transportation in comparison to their wages proved too great. On the Cape Flats, residents struggled to adjust to their changed circumstances and unfamiliar surroundings. The loss of homes, of neighbours and friends and of a place that held personal meaning would take years to overcome. Infrequent public transportation and a lack of shops intensified the strain of removal on people's lives. Adults were presented with challenges they thought they would not overcome. But over time, people did find within themselves an ability to carry on.

Ilford Investments applied for permission to erect a multi-storey apartment block in the area. The Council refused, as Tramway Road was considered too narrow. In 1963, bulldozers flattened the Tramway Road houses and those on the north side of Ilford Street.[15] The City of Cape Town landscaped a park, reserved for whites only, which remains to the present day.

Memory, Reunion and Restitution

Ex-residents of Tramway Road and Ilford Street continue to remember life in their former neighbourhood in a variety of ways. At birthdays, weddings, funerals and during personal visits, memories of Tramway Road and Ilford Street drift into conversation and ex-residents cherish an unexpected meeting. The organisation of and participation in reunions and land restitution claims emphasises the power of the past. The story of an ex-Ilford Street resident's experience, years after forced removal, shows the potent effects of memory:

> Was I nine? Eight or nine. Because on the day, the last day. School. I'll never forget that. I think that was the most traumatic. I never realised how traumatic it was until one day I did a psychodrama workshop ... We had to depict a scene in our life when I was about between one and ten [clears throat]. And I chose to to to play out role-play this day ... When I. Ja ... this is the night, when the [Tramway Road] school closed we had this celebration ... And because I used to ... every morning I had to

Pamela Peterson in her Tramway Road School uniform, ca. 1945

(District Six Museum)

Tramway Road reunion in Woodstock Town Hall, 1985

(District Six Museum)

> fill ... every Monday morning ... the principal's jug of water ... And I, oh yes! The night of this event, I, of course, was chosen to give, to hand over the bouquet of flowers. This vase. And then I remembered that. I remembered that and I'll never forget that night. That day when I wept. I wept like a baby ... [during the] psychodrama ... I mean that time I was too small to really understand. I think it was more excitement this movement and and all the different things were happening ... But anyway, there I am sitting with this. (Mrs C.C.)

The final day of school was a happy one. Yet, the full significance of this event and the underlying sadness and grief only began to surface years later. On an intensely personal level, these suppressed childhood memories reveal the extent of the emotional trauma and psychological costs of forced removals.

During the apartheid State of Emergency, ex-residents valued time with each other at a public site rather than seek security in their own homes. In March 1985, ex-residents reunited in the Woodstock Town Hall, to celebrate their past, their lives and their accomplishments. Former residents embraced each other, reminisced, enjoyed supper and danced. 'Casspirs patrolled the street outside but no one wanted to go home' (Mr L.L.).[16] 'It was really wonderful to come and meet all the people again. But that was just for those few hours' (Mr Ab.P.).

In 1996, ex-Tramway Road resident Mr L.L. initiated a meeting with former neighbours and ex-residents of Ilford Street to apply for land restitution. There are various reasons why residents want to or do not want to return. Mrs K.F. said, 'I got used to now staying here you know, quiet and so on ... It's not nice to move. Oh! It's terrible job moving. Things gets broken, packing in.' Mr A.J., who lived in Ilford Street, chose to remain in Bonteheuwel.

NOTICE 1259 OF 1996

GENERAL NOTICE IN TERMS OF THE RESTITUTION OF LAND RIGHTS ACT, 1994 (ACT No. 22 OF 1994)

Notice is hereby given in terms of section 12 (4) of Restitution of Land Rights Act, 1994 (Act No.22 of 1994), that the final date of 30 November 1996 for the lodgement of restitution claims for Sea Point (Tramway Road), Cape Town is hereby fixed. This is to make sure that the resources of the Commission or the Court would be more effectively utilised if all claims for restitution in respect of the land, or area or township in question, were to be investigated at the same time. Accordingly all potential claimants are invited to lodge their claims for the restitution of land rights in Sea Point (Tramway Road), Cape Town by not later than the abovementioned date.

The Commission on Restitution of Land Rights
Private Bag X9163
CAPE TOWN
8000.
Tel.(021) 26-2930.
Fax(021) 26-2702.

Note:
Please note that this notice applies only to those people who have not yet lodged their claim with the Commission.

W.A.MGOQI,
Deputy Chief Land Claims Commissioner.

A copy of the land restitution claim for ex-Tramway Road residents, 1996

(District Six Museum)

Mrs D.B.

Mrs D.B.'s paternal grandparents lived at 8 Tramway Road. When her parents got married, they rented a room in a cottage and then moved to 7 Tramway Road. A maternal aunt lived in 8 Tramway Road. Mrs D.B. was born in 1931. Her mother washed laundry for hotels, hair salons and restaurants. Her father drove a lorry for the Union Castle shipping line.

Mrs D.B. began her education at the Tramway Road School. Although she was a bright student at St Paul's School in the Bo-Kaap, she left school in Standard Six (Grade Eight) to work. 'All my friends were working and I wanted to follow them.' As a youngster, Mrs D.B. belonged to the Sunbeams. She also participated in the choir at St Paul's School, the Young People's Fellowship at the Holy Redeemer Church and the Eoan Group in Walmer Estate.

After forced removal to Bonteheuwel, to give her children guidance, Mrs D.B. organised her house to accommodate her children's needs. She encouraged her sons to play for the Sea Point Swifts, the soccer team that Tramway Road residents transplanted to the Cape Flats. 'Sometimes my house, this front room used to be a games room. I didn't want them to wander around the street. I had to let them play inside. They could play their cards, dominoes, darts. Whatever games they like and they liked soccer. They joined the Sea Point Swifts ... Weekends their father used to take them out fishing because they came from Sea Point. I told Mr B. straight: "Don't think because I come to live here in Bonteheuwel that you're going to keep me away from the sea." '

To be honest with you it's quite worse than the time when we stayed there. Quite worse. You not, you not safe at night there. No, I won't go back. Even if they offer me a place there. You got to re-establish yourself over again and get used to the people staying there, you know. The environment, you know, as they say.

Since 1961, a variety of events have brought about remarkable changes in Sea Point. People no longer feel the same familiarity with the suburb. People who have been putting down roots in Bonteheuwel for over thirty years mark this township as home, now with its own memories. Ex-residents who intend to return to Tramway Road do not know how they will pay for housing that will have to be built. Still, the wish to return to the place of memory spurs them on. When asked if she wanted to go back to Tramway Road, Ms C.K. replied:

Yes! I would like to, you know I used to because that's what I usually tell my daughter. I used to say to them. You know now, you don't know what life is ... we used to know the flowers and that ... we used to have different things to do at different times ... we used to go to the mountain ... If we want a different spot we go and ... go to the beach.

A generation not born in Tramway Road hears and reads selected memories that emphasise the wealth of the past compared to a seemingly poorer present. Memories of activities on the mountain and at the sea, taken for granted at the time, highlight the meaning of life and leisure in Tramway Road. These memories demonstrate a time that allowed for choice, satisfaction and companionship with friends. There is no doubt that forced removals challenged residents to re-orient their lives in profound ways.

As they were living in such a small, contained pocket in the heart of Sea Point, residents created neighbourhood networks. These helped them to survive in a society marked by segregation and apartheid. Public activities shaped the community, giving residents a sense of belonging and a sense of self. At the same time, social boundaries within and between the neighbourhoods reflected broader class and racial prejudices.

A small group of 40 Tramway Road residents are in the process of negotiating with the Land Claims Commission for the return of their land, now a vacant Council park. Another 115 former residents are claiming financial compensation. With the land now valued at four million rands, there are many vested interests involved. This has slowed down the process of restitution and former residents fear that their plan to return is only a pipe dream. 'We have done all our homework, we want to be role players, but we can't move forward.'[17] Should the time occur when ex-residents build homes where the park is now situated, Tramway Road will begin anew.

5 'Ja! So was District Six! But it was a beautiful place': Oral Histories, Memory and Identity

Felicity Swanson and Jane Harries

Your memories live longer than your dreams. Memories never fade if you got a good memory. But dreams fade ... If I could put the clock back! Those years will never come back again. But if you have memories like me, you can't be lonely, because you have your memories. (Mrs J.G.)[1]

At times it was a place of violence. But mostly it was a place of love, tolerance and kindness, a place of poverty and often of degradation, but a place where people had the intelligence to take what life gave them and give it meaning.[2]

The area known as District Six, situated close to the inner-city centre of Cape Town on the lower slopes of Devil's Peak, commands spectacular views of Table Mountain, the harbour and the sea. Castle Bridge, Sir Lowry Road, Searle Street and Walmer Estate mark out its physical boundaries. But District Six is much more than a geographical or residential space.

The 'District' has come to embody a collective

View from the slopes of Table Mountain over District Six and the Harbour, ca. 1960

(District Six Museum)

memory of home, family, neighbourliness and, above all, community. Former residents have a deep sense of belonging and identity that has since found creative expression in music, plays, poetry, literature and art. While apartheid's social engineering physically destroyed District Six, it did not succeed in erasing the place from popular memory.[3] As a former resident prophesied in 1966, 'You can take the place out of District Six, *ou pellie* [old friend], but you'll never take District Six out of the heart of the people.'[4] District Six has become a place of symbolic meaning, a memorial to all South Africans dispossessed by apartheid.

The greater part of District Six was formally proclaimed an area of white settlement on 11 February 1966, in accordance with the Group Areas Act of 1950. At this time it was the largest suburb in Cape Town, as well as one of the oldest. Densely populated and overcrowded, it was very similar in nature to other inner-city areas such as the Left Bank of Paris, the East End of London and the Bronx in New York.[5] It had become renowned for the cosmopolitan mix of its residents, a melting pot of cultures including people descended from freed slaves, Africans, European immigrants from Ireland and Jews from Eastern Europe. Over fifteen years, some 60 000 people were uprooted from their homes, which were demolished from 1968 onwards. By the early 1980s, with only a few mosques and churches left untouched by the bulldozers, the area was reduced to a wasteland of rubble and weeds.[6]

This is a brief history that aims to tell the stories of ordinary people who once lived in District Six. Schoolteachers, domestic workers, factory workers, seamstresses, nurses and housewives have contributed their oral recollections of the past. This essay is about their memories of everyday life in the years between the Second World War and their uprooting and dispersal to the distant townships of the Cape Flats after 1966.

District Six: From Kanaladorp to Inner-City Heartland

In the early 1800s the area that later became known as District Six formed part of the wine estates Welgelegen, Bloemhof, Zonnebloem and Hope Lodge. In subsequent years these farms were subdivided into 'garden houses', which were occupied by Dutch-speaking whites. Following the emancipation of slaves in 1834, a sizeable number of ex-slaves settled in the undeveloped areas.[7] As the economy and population of Cape Town expanded, many people settled in District Six. When the first municipality was established in 1840, the area was named District Twelve. In 1867

Smart Street, District Six

(South African Library)

Demolition: the final phase, 1980

(South African Library)

Cape Town was divided into six districts, and this area – originally called Kanaladorp by its inhabitants – was officially renamed District Six in this year.[8] Kanaladorp could be a reference to the canal on the eastern side of the district, but a more popular interpretation is that it was derived from the Malay word *kanala*, meaning 'to do a favour'.[9]

With the development of the railway in the 1860s and 1870s, the more affluent residents of District Six moved out to newer suburbs such as Observatory, Gardens, Green Point and Sea Point. The area suffered from continuing neglect at the hands of the municipality, which was unwilling to spend money on upgrading much-needed services such as sewerage, safe drinking water and roads. High-density terraced housing was generally substandard, with landlords unwilling to make improvements. These poor conditions and the overcrowding led to a smallpox epidemic in 1882. In 1901 some cases of bubonic plague were reported in the District and this was used as an opportunity to remove the Africans who were living there to Ndabeni.[10]

Because of its strategic and scenic position, District Six was highly valued and regarded as 'prime real estate', leaving it vulnerable to projects of 'urban renewal' and 'slum clearance'. These projects meant clearing out inhabitants of densely populated areas within city centres or within close proximity to commerce and industry. In 1940, the Cape Town City Council proposed the elimination of District Six in the interests of slum clearance and proposed an ambitious town-planning scheme.[11] The City Engineer wrote in 1940:

> One must not lose sight of the fact that the District is capable of being one of the finest in the city, as it at one time was, before being allowed to deteriorate. Centrally situated, and to become more central with the new foreshore developments, it is a healthy site and commands a magnificent outlook. Today it is a blot in a beautiful city and a disgrace to civilised conceptions of how human beings should live.[12]

It is clear that this period marked the beginning of the end of District Six, during which urban renewal plans served to conceal segregationist policies and the interests of big business.[13]

Street Life and Popular Culture

By 1966, District Six was a densely populated suburb. It was almost exclusively a working-class community and most residents were coloured Capetonians. While many outsiders regarded District Six as an overcrowded slum harbouring criminal elements and gang members, the majority of people living there were law-abiding citizens' with deeply rooted family and community ties and a strong sense of belonging.[14]

> District Six was a cosmopolitan place. We all stayed together – Germans, so-called whites, blacks, people from Indonesia and Malaysia, Irish people like my Gran, all those stayed together and needless of colour ... and we mixed. We had a beautiful relationship. Here there was no need ... near to the shops, near to the market, near to the fish, schools were there. (Mrs R.T.)

Community infrastructures were well established. There were over twenty schools and colleges, including the well-known Trafalgar and Harold Cressy high schools. Eighteen churches, three mosques and four synagogues served the community, indicating that there was a good degree of religious tolerance.[15] The Lieberman Institute was built in 1934 and together with the Marion Institute provided the community with important cultural centres. Woodstock beach was a short walk away, the mountain on the doorstep. It was a quick bus ride to Sea Point and Green Point. Many people were able to walk to work at the harbour, or to the city centre or the factories in the neighbouring suburbs of Woodstock and Salt River.

Hanover Street was the heart of District Six. It was here that social activity, entertainment and trading took place. People of 'all colours and creeds' lived side by side in Hanover Street, 'select people, average families, and gangsters all lived next to each other, and all hung their washing

View from District Six over Cape Town after the Group Areas Act

(University of Cape Town Libraries/Manuscripts and Archives)

Second Circle Girl Guides,
Marion Institute, ca. 1950

(South African Library)

Pupils at Ashley Street School

(South African Library)

The Star bioscope at 158 Hanover Street in 1948

(South African Library)

from the buildings'.[16] There was a variety of well-known shops such as the Globe Furnishing Company, Shrands and Maxims shoe shops, Waynicks clothing store, the Little Wonder Store, Van de Schyff's dress material store, and Janjira's grocery shop. The area was also served by barbers, hairdressers, the fish market, the Star and Avalon bioscopes, butchers, hotels, cafés, and the Rose and Crown and Cheltenham pubs. Hawkers sold their fruit and vegetables from their barrows, horse-carts or *bakkies* (vans). Shopkeepers displayed a variety of colourful goods outside their shops, packing the pavements with racks of shoes, handbags, clothes and household goods. Day and night it was a vibrant, noisy, energetic place. 'Hanover Street ... a river of people, cars, barrows, buses, horse-drawn carts and small boys racing down slopes in soap box carts: a bustling, laughing, hooting, whistling, shouting, chatting river of people.'[17]

In a similar vein, novelist and former resident Alex La Guma depicts evening street life in and around Hanover Street:

Up ahead the music shops were still going full blast, the blare of records all mixed up so you could not tell one from the other. Shopkeepers, Jewish, Indian, and Greek, stood in doorways along the arcade of stores on each side of the street, waiting to welcome last minute customers: and the vegetable and fruit barrows were still out too, the hawkers

in white coats yelling their wares and flapping their brown paper packets, bringing prices down now that the day was ending.[18]

Given the harsh realities of low wages, seasonal work and unemployment, the numerous smaller local grocery shops provided a lifeline to many poor families trying to make ends meet. They sold essential items such as fish oil, jam, sugar, tea and coffee in small quantities. People could afford the few pennies or cents charged for a tablespoon of jam or a small glass of fish oil. Goods could also be bought on credit. These groceries were owned by Indian, Malay and Jewish shopkeepers or *handelaars*, who sold a variety of delicious foods that reflected this ethnic mix. According to one resident, 'The *Rooikop Jood* [Red-headed Jew] was our favourite shop. The tall good-looking shopkeeper and his assistants knew all their customers by name ... they also knew what brand of item to give to which families. He was famous for his delicious *snoekmootjies*, thick pieces of raw snoek pickled in vinegar and spices.'[19] In the predominantly Jewish area around Harrington, Albertus and Buitenkant Streets, there was a man called *Jood Brood* (the Bread Jew), who ran a small bakery selling fresh bread rolls, *kitke* (a traditional Jewish loaf) and rye bread every morning.[20] The Indian and Malay or *babbie* shops were, in turn, renowned for their fragrant spices, curries, *roti* (flat bread), *samoosas* (fried pastries with meat or vegetable filling), *dhaltjies* (chilli bites) and *koeksisters* (a sweet dough, fried and soaked in syrup).

With landlords and the municipality unwilling to upgrade housing, many neighbourhoods in District Six were run-down and neglected. Influential writers Alex La Guma and Richard Rive, who were both raised in District Six, are

Street life in District Six, 1948

(South African Library)

Wagon-making in District Six

(University of Cape Town Libraries/Manuscripts and Archives)

harsh and unsentimental in their assessment of the living conditions. They portray a world of dirty, smelly, garbage-filled alleys and streets and broken-down, damp, overcrowded buildings and dark, depressing rooms.[21] Mrs S.N., a midwife assisting at a home delivery late one rainy night, had first-hand experience of this:

> I remember delivering one night. It was pouring with rain. It must have been two or three families sharing one room ... I can remember having to chase the whole lot, all the men outside. And then the woman in the double bed with last year's baby next to her and the year before next to that, one sticking out at the bottom of the bed. And down in the corner were mattresses with about five little kids all with their eyes wide open. I can just remember all those eyes all looking. It was nothing very private.

Mrs S.N. recognised that District Six was a 'place of terrific contrasts'. 'There were some really beautiful, very nice homes, and there were some very bad slums as well. Despite the poverty and often poor living conditions District Six was a community.'

Hanover Street wash house

(University of Cape Town Libraries/Manuscripts and Archives)

Polliack's Music Store, Hanover Street, 1905

(South African Library)

POLLIACKS ORIGINAL MUSIC STORE AT 15 HANOVER STREET, CAPE TOWN, PHOTOGRAPHED IN 1903 AND ESTABLISHED BY Mʀ A. POLLIACK AT THE SAME ADDRESS IN THE YEAR 1896.

Other residents have more positive memories. Ms L.F. and her family rented a semi-detached cottage in Tyne Street (known by the locals as 'Tiny' Street), part of a row of terraced houses. With its distinctive flat roof, sash windows, wooden shutters, *stoep* (verandah) and decorative fanlight above the front door, it was similar in style to those in the Malay Quarter of the Bo-Kaap. It was home to a large family of eleven and consisted of a long passage, two rooms, a kitchen and a backyard. At the time of forced removals her mother and aunt had lived there for over sixty years. Ms L.F. remembers that 'we all got on each other's nerves because of a general lack of privacy'. But despite all this, it was a home that provided family stability.[22]

Many African families lived in District Six. At the time of the removals in the 1960s, over seventy families were living in the area of Cross, Hanover, Horstley, Constitution and Reform Streets. Ms N.N. was born at the local Peninsula Maternity Home and grew up in Cross Street. Her family of six rented one room in a double-storey building owned by a Muslim landlord. In 1961 the rent was one rand and ten cents per month. Her father worked in a factory in Woodstock, her mother did domestic work. The building was occupied by African tenants, one family to each room. These arrangements were tightly controlled to keep tensions down to a minimum:

A social worker visits a District Six family

(University of Cape Town Libraries/Manuscripts and Archives)

There was a communal kitchen, and it was in this kitchen that the families met to formulate rules for the group of tenants. The families shared the same washing lines, the same outside toilet, one rubbish bin, and one postbox. It was therefore necessary for the group to draw up some rules so as to avoid friction and conflict. The rules stated very plainly the days on which each family had to clean the toilet, take out the rubbish bin, open the letterbox and hand over the mail to the relevant people, could use the washing line, and so forth. This resulted in perfect harmony and tolerance.[23]

In the 1950s Ms N.N. attended the only school for African children in District Six. This was the junior primary school at the Methodist Church Hall in Chapel Street.

School was quite a social place, because we had the opportunity of meeting other black children. The black children lived spread out amongst the coloured and other families in District Six, and as most grown-ups worked outside District Six, our parents mostly met one another through the friends we made at school. Some children came from farther afield – from Bo-Kaap and Woodstock, because there was only one school for black children in central Cape Town, and it only went up to Standard Two [Grade Four].

Because of the Nationalist government's policies of separate education, black children were not allowed to attend coloured schools.

During the early 1950s, separate education was provided for 'natives' and coloureds and unless someone 'changed' their identity they stayed with their group. Because most of our parents did not want us to lose our identity, we were all sent to the Methodist School in Chapel Street.[24]

The overcrowded living conditions and the lack of open public spaces made for a communal street life where meeting friends and children playing on the streets was part of the social fabric of the area:

> District Six was a high-density area. There were very few recreational facilities. There were very few parks, and very few places where children could play, besides the homes were very small. There were no sitting rooms or lounges. A room might be a sitting room by day but at night it would be converted into a bedroom. So there was not much space in the home. So children were compelled to spend their leisure activities outside the home except on rainy days ... On every street corner in District Six there, there was not one shop, but two or even three. Because children did not have much space in their homes, they would go and play outside and the street corner would be the spot where the groups would meet. To every street corner a group was attached. We used the term *hoek hou* and even today people will say *Ons het by daardie, of by daardie hoek, hoek gehou.* It means in fact that they came together and socialised on that spot or corner. (Mr C.B.)

Gangs: Heroes and Villains

The notorious gangs of District Six were very much part of this street culture and seem to have become prominent after the Second World War.[25] According to Mr B.D, '[t]here was a lot of gangs, there was about, in what, in about a kilometre square you will get five or six gangs in that square kilometre'. There were various gangs such as the Killers, the Jesters, the Red Cats, the Rangers

and the Globe Gang. The Globes initially started as a vigilante group, taking their name from the Globe Furnishing Company in Hanover Street. Members were drawn from old District Six families, shopkeepers, craftsmen and traders whose security was threatened. By the 1950s they were involved in extortion, blackmail, gambling, smuggling, shebeens and dealing in stolen goods.[26]

Gangs were very territorial, none more so than the Seven Steps gang, whose 'headquarters' were the now legendary Seven Steps.

> *Seven Steps! Nou daai was ook 'n gang. Daar het ook gestaan boys ... Seven Steps, nou dit was so 'n lyn ... en dan was daar sewe steppies op en*

The legendary Seven Steps

(South African Library)

*dan loop jy die lyn op en dan kom jy die
anderkant van Caledon Straat. This is Hanover
Street, hier is die Seven Steps. Nou hier was 'n
Indian Shop, Sabadiens. Nou loop jy op die Sewe
Steps, en dan is dit so 'n klipperigge paadjie op
soos 'n avenue en dan loop jy daar af na die
ander pad. Daai was Sewe Steps! Die Sewe Steps
boys, hulle het so hoeke gehou, man.* [Seven
Steps! Now, that was also a gang. The boys
used to hang around ... Seven Steps, now,
there was this line and then there were seven
steps up and then you walk this line and then
you come to the other side of Caledon Street.
This is Hanover Street, here are the Seven
Steps. Now there was an Indian shop,
Sabadiens. Now, as you walk up the Seven
Steps and it is a cobbled path like a lane and
then you walk down there and you reach the
other road. That was Seven Steps! The Seven
Steps boys, they were always hanging around
at that corner, man.] (Mrs A.)

But most residents describe the gangs as not
really interfering with or threatening people who
were part of the community. 'The gangs did not
interfere with people from Hanover Street. They
fight on each other. But not with decent people,
no! They drank and smoke *dagga* [marijuana] but
they didn't interfere with good people' (Mr C.B.).
Mrs G.J. describes them as gentleman gangs: 'They
weren't dressed like gangsters or *skollies* [hooli-
gans]. They wore suits and ties. They were dressed
to kill, they wore hats as well, like the Mafia. But
those gangsters, they didn't fight with the people,
they just fight amongst themselves.'

District Six was depicted as a safe place in contrast to the townships, where many of these people were relocated. Mr A.D's description of gangs
active in District Six in the 1950s confirms that
District Six was not always as violent as it was portrayed by the media and the government. Gangs
frequently warned residents ahead of time of their
intended activities.

I don't think District Six was as violent as it
was made out to be. My own impressions
were that it was surprisingly non-violent.
Then gangs were gang fights, not involving
the ordinary citizen in the street. The gangs
would send emissaries around saying 'we are
having the fights, off the streets'. In fact I
walked around District Six during this time
as a young man in the streets in 1966/1967
and was never robbed. I even walked around
Hanover Street between twelve and one
o'clock every night. (Mr A.D.)

Mrs G.J.

Mrs G.J. was born in 1926. As a young child she
lived with her aunt and uncle in District Six and
would visit her parents on weekends. From an
early age she was drawn to the Muslim faith. She
lived in a street in District Six that was predominantly Muslim. Most of her childhood friends
were Muslim girls and she went with them to
Muslim school. She knew her aunt and uncle
would be opposed to her converting to Islam, so
she sought permission from her father. Her
father's response was that he could not prevent
her but that once she made the decision to con-
vert to Islam she could not at a later stage revert
back to being a Christian. At the age of 18 she
converted from Christianity to Islam. Her aunt
and uncle disapproved of her conversion. As a
result she had to leave their home and went to
live with other relations.

She remained in District Six and soon
met and married her husband, who was also
from District Six. Her wedding was a 'simple
house wedding'. Her marriage was short-lived –
she was widowed at the youthful age of 22.
After her husband's death, she lived with her
mother-in-law. In order to support herself and
her two children, Mrs G.J. found work at a local
factory. She was reunited with her aunt when
her second child was born, yet continued to live
with her mother-in-law and has remained a
Muslim.

Mrs S.N., a midwife at the local Peninsula Maternity Hospital, recounts how she and her nursing friends were able to go to a local café late at night to buy cooldrinks and cigarettes and feel perfectly safe: 'We would walk down Constitution Street, there was a café just down Constitution Street and think nothing of it.'

Leisure Activities

Over the years the people of District Six developed their own unique forms of popular recreation and cultural life. Going to the cinema and participating in the New Year's Coon Carnival were unquestionably two of the most popular forms of entertainment in District Six. The local bioscope occupied a special position in the recreational life of the community, 'a place to which both adults and children went in order to be cocooned in the dream world of the flickering screen'.[27] The Avalon, Star, National, and the British bioscopes were generally affordable and easily accessible to residents. Many people recall the packed Saturday afternoon matinees, during which patrons were entertained by the latest episode of *Zorro*. The cinemas were also used to host beauty pageants, talent shows and musicals.

The Star bioscope was the cheapest of the cinemas and was divided into two sections, an upstairs and a downstairs. The downstairs was frequented by students and other young people, where the seats were cheaper, while the upstairs was reserved for more 'respectable' cinema viewers. To watch a film from upstairs at the Star was all right, but one had to be brave to sit downstairs.[28]

As you sit in the Star bioscope all the flies from the fish market goes in there. But that was a hell of a bioscope. They used to sell *dagga* inside. There's more smoke than people. When you come in then you smoke the *dagga*. When you come out your clothes stink like *dagga*. But it was lovely. They were very happy people. (Mr C.B.)

But not all patrons agreed with this assessment.

We never dared to use the back seats, because this part of the cinema would be occupied by the Globe gang. The members of the gang ... were *dagga* smokers. The heavy, pungent smoke that drifted from the back row irritated us a lot. It burnt our eyes and choked us, but the ushers never did anything about it.[29]

For Ms N.N. the Star was an easy five-minute walk from her home in Cross Street.

The Star was not as well organised as the Avalon, and you paid as you entered. This arrangement suited us fine because it meant that some of us could get in without paying. What we did was to give our money to Glad to buy all the tickets. We would then quickly rush in, telling the usher that the tickets were with Glad and that she was behind us. By the time he discovered that he had been tricked, we were safely inside. But they never really bothered to check on us, especially our favourite usher, Sakkie, who was kind and used to dealing with children. Anyway, we were old patrons.[30]

Going to the cinema was not merely about watching a particular film, it was also about having fun, meeting friends and acquaintances.

You could take anything into the Star you know, they just had wooden seats downstairs, so it was all right for fish and chips and other hot food. But not at the Avalon, no never at the Avalon. They had ushers there to check you and make you stand outside to eat food. The Avalon, you see, was a more respectable kind of bioscope, it was mostly the better class of person who went there. Although it was not much more to go in there than the Star. (Mrs I.G.)[31]

The New Year's Coon Carnival was an important annual event in the cultural life of District Six, celebrated by young and old, men and women. Community ties were strengthened through participation in the street carnival, which was a

Mr C.S.

Mr C.S. was born in 1938. His family moved to District Six when he was 7 years old. They initially lived in Hanover Street and then moved to the Bloemhof Flats. He attended Albertus Street Primary School, locally known as the school for the poor, or *die stye skooltjie*. His father worked as a waiter but did not earn enough to support his family so he was compelled to find work at the age of 12. His mother's family owned a fruit and vegetable stall on the Old Parade and he would work there every afternoon after school and all day on Saturdays. He would clean, sweep and pack away the empty boxes. He earned a few pennies every day and by the end of the week these would add up to a pound.

He attended Trafalgar High School. The school played a significant role in his professional life and in his decision to become a teacher. A particular teacher encouraged him and became a mentor. This teacher had a back problem and was unable to stand for long periods of time, so Mr C.S. took over writing on the blackboard, which he enjoyed very much. He completed school in 1956 and enrolled as a student teacher at Hewat Training College the following year. He continued to work at the fruit and vegetable stall until he completed his teacher training. The College was opposite Roeland Street jail behind Bloemhof Flats, where Harold Cressy School is situated today. He was thus fortunate that all his schooling and education was located right on his doorstep. He qualified as a teacher in 1958, and his first teaching position was at Douglas Road Primary School in Wynberg.

striking home-grown product of District Six. At the same time, the carnival was an expression of a working-class identity that was rooted in urban Cape Town.[32]

As dit Nuwe Jaar gewees het in die Kaap. Toe my ouma nog gelewe het, het my pa en ma hulle en drie, twee dae voor Ou Jaar, dan sit die mense hulle banke reg al. Hulle weet waar hulle sit. Dan maak die ouma sout vleise, gebakte broode, terte. Als maak hulle. Dan sal jy dink die mense gaan piekniek. Hulle piekniek sommer! My ouma woon daar oorkant. Dis in Hanover Straat. Dan sit sy sommer, net so hier op die hoek. Families, almal ken vir almal so jy kan nie honger gely het nie, want sy was die koeksister bakker op Tennantstraat se hoek. [When it was New Year in the Cape. When my grandmother was still alive, and my mother and father, two, three days before the old year, people put their benches out. They all know where to sit. My grandmother made corned meats, baked breads and pies. They made everything. You would think that they were going on a picnic. They just picnic there! My grandmother lived opposite. This is in Hanover Street. She just sat there on the corner. All the families knew each other, so you were never hungry, she was the *koeksister* baker of Tennant Street.] (Mr N.A.)

Former members speak of the enormous amount of enjoyment they got out of participating in the carnival. For them the carnival was a celebration of music, singing, marching and dancing as they owned the streets of Cape Town, if only for one day of the year.

I am telling you, it was, it's long ago, but when you look back, we should have had videos of all those years and we played back those years, compared to now ... I mean when you go to Hanover Street. Hah! I'm telling you, everybody sitting there on their *bankies* [benches], on their tins, waiting for the coons to come. I'm telling you, no it was lovely to be in the coons – it's a joyous affair, it's all got rhythm singing you know. And then *goema, goema, goema* [drumbeats], fantasia you know! (Mr A.S.)

Mr B.D. was involved with the coons from a very early age. As far as his grandmother was concerned, the many hours of practising and organisation that were required to be a coon member kept many youngsters busy and out of trouble.

The first time I was involved with the coons ... I was a child of about 3 years old. My mother used to walk with a baby's bottle behind the coons you see and you hear my brother with them, we are *jolling* [partying]. Some of them carried us, sometimes we walked, sometimes we ride because we are only babies. Actually then it was very nice! Every year. The people on corners, the corners are springing up like palm trees and everything. If you were a Starlite the colours would hang there. If you were a Pennsylvanian or if you were a Hanover, your colours will hang there. And they will have seats there, sitting there. They will sleep there, eat, because it's from New Year's Eve till the night is up and down ... you don't want to be a loser always [laughs]. Sometimes if you're about ten guys, like we were in District Six, and we sing on the street corners that time. You see, we know each

other's voice, then we all join one troupe, you see. We know how to sing, we know how we can fit our voices in, you see. That was before the brass come in. (Mr B.D.)

While women did not actually form part of the coon troupes, they played an important role in making the costumes for the singers and dancers and in baking for both participants and spectators. The carnival provided residents with an opportunity to have fun, to spend time away from work and to mix freely with neighbours. It also promoted a broader community consciousness that crossed religious and cultural differences.[33]

The Spirit of Kanaladorp: Community and Struggle

A common thread running through these oral stories is the sense of neighbourliness and community spirit. Poverty and the shared experiences of day-to-day hardships brought people together

---

Mr E.G.

Mr E.G. was born in the Bo-Kaap in 1925. After the death of his father, the family moved to Cross Street in District Six. His mother's income from washing and ironing was small, and times were hard for the family. He left school in Standard Five (Grade Seven) at the age of 12 and found work selling newspapers. He had to be up by 5 a.m. to sell the *Cape Times* on the corner of Plein and Roeland Streets and then go back again in the afternoon to sell the *Argus*. He was paid two shillings and sixpence for each dozen newspapers sold. Over the years he also found temporary employment as a messenger, a cleaner and as a golf caddie at the Metropolitan Golf Club in Green Point.

During the Second World War he joined the Cape Coloured Corps as a signaller in the artillery. When he was demobilised in 1946 he became a foreman at Metal Box. Today he is a lay pastor in the church.

Mr E.G's great passion in life was music. As a teenager in District Six, he was a member of the Diamond Eyes Coon Troupe and sang in the Young

Easter Stars Christmas Choir. He started a dance band called the Paramount Dixie Band and played the saxophone, banjo and accordion. Bandleaders would congregate at Alf Wiley's barber shop, where they were able to find dance jobs. His band wore black trousers with satin strips, blue tuxedos and maroon bowties. Mr E.G. wore a checked tuxedo with black satin cuffs and lapels, 'very, very dressified'. He was able to buy his first car, a Studebaker, for 80 pounds, and his band travelled all over the Cape Peninsula, performing in the evenings and on weekends. 'I tell you, you could never take music away from the Capetonians. Musicians, you could never take that away from Cape Town. No man! They played, man they played! They played with their whole heart, you know, with their soul man! I am not putting on anything, even now if I should play, you are always going like this, because I used to enjoy playing music, you know. That's now my only thing in life that I really loved. It was my hobby, that was my every thing. Music! I liked music.'

---

in many ways.[34] Street life on Constitution Street demonstrated this:

> On Sunday afternoons people would sit outside their houses. Now as you can imagine it's going uphill. If you sit in one spot you can see others sitting up the hill. People would sit on the pavement outside having tea and whoever comes around sits and just enjoys themselves. People would have watermelon sliced up and it would pass from this side up the road and whoever is sitting up there. And they would say 'send to those people up there and give to them across the road'. They were free and hospitable at that time. They would shout over there and have conversations with people about three or four houses away. Everyone would just chime in. (Mrs F.)

Ms N.N. describes this community solidarity, where a deep sense of kinship shaped the social relationships between the residents of District Six, as *ubuntu*. In a community where regular employment was never secure, money was often scarce.

> Every Friday afternoon we were sent to fetch fruit and vegetables. When we got to the market we would find the bags ready for us to take home, and not a single penny was spent. Bhut' Gosa gave us fruit, Tat'u gave us cabbage and carrots, then from Bhut' Michael we collected potatoes and onions.[35]

Mr O.A. recalls how generous everyone was in their crowded tenement block.

> [A]s my ma poeding gemaak het, en soe aan, en dan, moet ek dit na die different kamers gaan gee. En die ou wat daar gewoon het, hy het gewerk in die docks. En dan bring hy sakke van stokvis. Eers was die stokvis baie cheap gewees. En dan bring hy stokvis, sakke stokvis, né ... en dan kry my ma ook. Ek kan onthou hoe my ma het frikkadelle en so aan ... grote, grote bakke frikkadelle. En daaityd die kreef was so cheap gewees ... dit was nie fyn doppies soos nou nie. Dit was groot doppe gewees. En groot pote ...

> Dan maak my ma nou eers kreef kerrie van die pote en doppe en so aan. En soe het ons aangegaan. En nou so het ons lewe in die Kaap. My pa het min geld verdien. En ons het nooit sonder kos gewees nie. Ons het nooit sonder kos gaan slaap nie. [When my mother made pudding, and so on, then I would take some to the different rooms. And that man who lived there, he worked in the docks. And then he brings sacks of ... stockfish. Stockfish was very cheap then. And then he brings sackloads of stockfish and my mother also gets some. And I remember how my mother had fishcakes ... big, big basins of fishcakes. And in those days crayfish was so cheap ... it was not the small shells that you get now. They were big shells. And big legs ... Then my mother made crayfish curry from the shells and legs and so on. And so we went on. This is how we lived in the Cape. My father earned very little money. And we were never without food. We never went to bed hungry.]

Neighbourhood solidarity based on common circumstances and tolerant attitudes of 'live and let live' seems to have overcome racial prejudices as well. Mr C.S. said:

> There was quite a number of Africans staying in District Six. We had no hang-ups about them being African. It was only people in the suburbs. They were a bit conscious. But in District Six there was no thought like that about Africans. If you're a person, you're a person – especially if you are a ballroom dancer. Everyone regards you as a person. Colour or religion, or creed never came into it. Until the fifties, then there was a snag and the coloureds formed a separate ballroom association, the Coloured Ballroom Association.

The realities of apartheid were felt more sharply outside the area. When she was a young woman, Mrs G.J. experienced racial discrimination prior to the advent of the Group Areas Act. She recalls how because of 'all the mixing in District Six' residents were unaware of many of the daily realities of segregation. She remembers how she used to play in Greenhaven Park near Roeland Street.

> We used to go to the park and we would play in the park. No European people ever chased us away ... They were happy days, they were nice times. That time the European people, coloured people, black people all mixed. There was no argument about it, such as 'you can't sit here, you can't sit there'. On the benches you know. Then afterwards they marked all that. This is for Europeans, this is for coloureds. They even marked the benches even on the station. I can remember one day I went to the station. I was quite big, 15 or 16, so I just went to sit, as I was tired. There was me and another girl and we just sat down – and then those people the railway police ... It wasn't coloureds then, it was all *boere*.[36] Get up, bladdy *Hotnots*, look where you sit.[37] Stand up! And I got such a fright and the other girl, that I just ran. From opposite the Parade I just ran up Darling Street and I go home ... We didn't know that time apartheid was in. Children didn't know what apartheid means, it was first segregation before apartheid. Then when all this came in they made it apartheid. We just got to know that. This policeman said: *Hey, weet jy waar jy sit?* [Hey, do you know where you are sitting?] He said it like that. Man, and there the train came in and it was full, full of European people and I felt embarrassed. I felt so ashamed. I just ran. I was so frightened. I was scared.

This incident left her feeling helpless and guilty for 'doing nothing, merely for sitting on a bench'. Later at home she had time to reflect on what had occurred and felt extremely angry.

District Six was a hive of political activity, a place where many leaders and intellectuals who opposed apartheid and the government either lived or congregated. Political activists such as Cissy Gool, Dr Abdurahman, Ben Kies and eminent writers such as Alex La Guma and Richard Rive all hailed from District Six. Former resident Mr V.K. argues that the Nationalist government was threatened by this activism that cut across racial and ethnic divides:

> I'd say District Six, if ever there was a reason why District Six had to be destroyed it was because of the quality of the thinking in the area. The whole cultural mix was something they couldn't handle, this cosmopolitan mix. This kind of East End mix, Jew, Arab and Christians lived in one street. That was their philosophy and that had to be destroyed. District Six is the tail end of apartheid, I mean Soweto and Sophiatown was destroyed long before that.

Memory and Identity: 'Ja! So was District Six! But it was a beautiful place'

The implementation of the Group Areas Act in 1966 was a traumatic turning point for the people of District Six. The physical destruction of homes and businesses brought with it untold social and economic costs and widespread insecurity. Many residents felt a strong sense of belonging and identity as *mense van die Kaap* (Capetonians) that was connected to the physical space of District Six. People experienced a loss of a common heritage when they were displaced to the townships, as their close ties to the mother city were broken.

> *En as ons op onse stoepe staan en dan het ons die hele Table Mountain gesien. En as ons in die backyard staan en dan sien ons die hele docks. Soe lekker het ons gewoon. En ons wil nie uit nie, ons wil nie net gemove het nie. Maar dis was really lekker gewees om in die Kaap te bly. Homely en lekker bymekaar gebly.* [And if we stood on our verandahs, then we could see the whole of Table Mountain. And if we stood in the backyard, we could see the whole of the docks. And it was really nice to live there. We did not want to move out. But it was really nice to stay in the Cape. Homely and nice to stay there.] (Mrs A.)

Removals truck in Frere Street

(District Six Museum)

The Bristol Barber, 1980

(South African Library)

Many people were angry and bitter after being forced out of District Six. They felt disconnected from their urban roots, cast out into the unfamiliar world of the townships on the windswept Cape Flats, almost in the biblical sense of being sent into exile. 'And then the people had to move out. They were brought into this Cape Flats. It was a barren land. There was nothing' (Mr K.T.).

The less tangible emotional and psychological costs were as severe, as important family, neighbourhood and community networks disintegrated. This is reflected in the personal memories of many people who in their stories recreate District Six as a secure and familiar world.

There will never come another place like District Six. There were very good people and there were fair people ... District Six was a nice place, it was a lovely place. Better than here – it's better. This government will never

Dover Street

(South African Library)

build another District Six. Oh! There will never be another District Six ... people were happy in District Six until ... the Group Areas. Now people must move to that side – put to that side. But so far there was not a place like District Six ... I miss District Six. I am every Friday there in District Six. I go early, seven o'clock, quarter to seven I leave here. Then I go to the barber, talk a little there and then I go into the mosque. Ja! So was District Six! But it was a beautiful place. Here everybody's for themselves. They don't worry with nobody. It was a happy family that stayed in District Six. Everybody knew from everybody. And then if there is any trouble, they come together quickly, not like here. They were all together. Muslim, Christian, Jewish and Indians. (Mr C.B.)

Perceptions and memories slip back and forth between nostalgia for a lost golden age free from conflict to the present harsh realities. These romanticised images obscure the contradictions of District Six. As many sources have shown, District

Mrs Z.B.

Mrs Z.B. was born in 1903. Her father was a merchant and importer and owned his own company. He was born in India, grew up in Mauritius and came to Cape Town at the age of 17. Her mother was a Muslim from Cape Town. As a young child Mrs Z.B. attended the Anglican Mission School in Roeland Street. Although both Muslim and Christian children were educated there, the emphasis was on Christian education. She learnt Arabic from a private teacher in Hanover Street. In primary school her teachers were all white women, and she remembers how strict and formal they were.

From Standard Four (Grade Six) she attended Trafalgar High School, where there was far more interaction between staff members and students and she felt very much a part of the school community. She passed matric and went on to the University of Fort Hare, where she completed an arts degree in 1928 and then obtained a teacher's diploma at Zonnebloem College in Cape Town. Her academic success caused 'a lot of talk' in the Muslim community, as it was unusual for a woman to become so educated. As a coloured person it was difficult for her to find employment at this time and she eventually taught in primary schools despite her extensive qualifications.

She experienced discrimination long before the apartheid years. Members of the coloured community had to apply for concessions in order to attend performances at the opera house in Darling Street. At the Tivoli Theatre, seating for coloureds was restricted to the gallery. She has vivid memories of her childhood, when she and her family travelled in a horse and cart to picnic in Claremont or Constantia. She would also accompany her mother on shopping expeditions to department stores such as Fletcher and Cartwrights, Stuttafords and Garlicks.

Six was seldom such a peaceful and harmonious community. Crime and violence were part of everyday life and gangsters were not the harmless rogues portrayed in these recollections.[38] Although black residents were the first group to be moved out under the Act, the community did not voice opposition to it. There is no doubt that poverty, overcrowding, competition over scarce resources and violence existed alongside neighbourliness and community solidarity. Tensions and conflicts in the community are largely silenced in these stories as only the positive aspects are remembered.

The destruction of District Six was a difficult and painful turning point in the lives of everyone involved. Memories provide a way of coming to terms with a past that was filled with hardship. The strength of District Six in popular memory is that the act of remembering is a coping strategy for the present.[39] As Mr V.K. explains, 'In many respects District Six is about memory, identity, ownership and politics, a kaleidoscope of people, events and experiences. But memory is often selective. One always remembers and passes on the positive memories to one's children.'[40] It is through memory that people are able to create meaning and sustain a positive sense of personal and community identity.[41]

The community of District Six no longer exists. Today, it is a place that remains an 'open wound' on the city landscape.[42] The memories recorded here provide important links between past residents and present generations. They serve as a reminder of just how much the city of Cape Town has lost in terms of its cultural heritage. But perhaps more importantly, these positive images of District Six expose the harsh injustices of apartheid. The history of District Six and forced removals are very much part of the broader history of the struggle against racism, prejudice and segregation in South Africa. As Richard Rive writes, 'It is now a mark of social prestige to "have come out of that".'[43]

6 'It changed everybody's lives': The Simon's Town Group Areas Removals[1]

Albert Thomas

Situated about forty-five kilometres from Cape Town at the end of the suburban railway network, Simon's Town is the southernmost town of the Cape Peninsula. The town nestles in the curve of False Bay, occupying the whole of Simon's Bay, with a steep mountain range covering its back. It is protected by this natural environment from the twin wind-devils of the southeasters of summer and the northwesters of winter. Any understanding of the history of Simon's Town must take into account the 'background of wind and weather'.[2]

From Murdoch Valley in the south to Glencairn in the north and over the Red Hill mountains, coloured people had settled there for more than two centuries. At the time of forced removals in 1967, Simon's Town had developed into a bustling naval town. It was a predominantly coloured community with smaller African and white communities. The vast majority of the

A view of False Bay and Simon's Town, ca. 1900

(Simon's Town Museum)

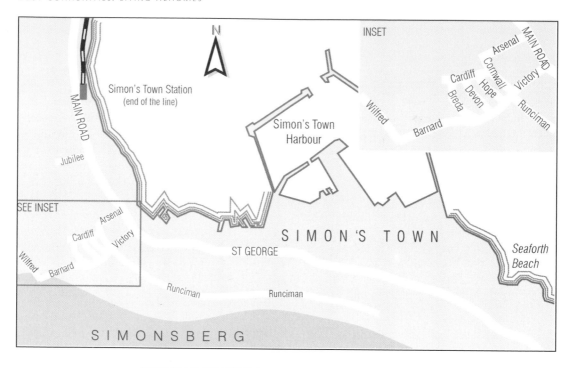

Simon van der Stel,
Governor of the Cape
Colony, 1679-1699

(Simon's Town Museum)

coloured communi-
ty of Simon's Town
lived in Council
houses in the Kloof
and Dido Valley
areas. Large pockets
were also scattered throughout the town. When
the notorious Group Areas Act was used to declare
Simon's Town a whites-only area in 1967, people
were shocked and could not believe that they
would be removed from a place where, for so
many generations, they had lived undisturbed.
This chapter is based on an oral history research
project started in 1995 and deals specifically with
the application of the Group Areas Act as it affected the coloured community of Simon's Town in
the late 1960s.[3]

Simon's Town: Historical Background

It all started in May 1671, when the Dutch flute
Isselsteijn was forced into False Bay to escape the
notorious winds of the Cape.[4] The Dutch crew also
required fresh water and meat, which they
bartered against tobacco and copper from the local
Khoikhoi. The bay in which they sought refuge
was named Isselsteijn Bay. The captain of the
Isselsteijn reported favourably to the Dutch East
India Company in Batavia of the merits of this bay
as a winter anchorage. The authorities never forgot
these recommendations and in 1687 Simon van
der Stel undertook a thorough exploration of False
Bay using Isselsteijn Bay as his base. This exploration became necessary because of the winter
winds which blew the Dutch ships onto the
beaches of Table Bay. The Company instructed
Van der Stel to find a winter anchorage nearby for
their ships. Van der Stel renamed Isselsteijn Bay
after himself and later, when the town was established, it was also named after him. A permanent
winter harbour was established in 1743 by Baron

von Imhoff, the Governor-General of Dutch possessions in the East Indies.

It was during this time that the coloured community of Simon's Town grew. As in the rest of the Western Cape, coloured people were descendants of the indigenous peoples, the Khoisan, European settlers and slaves from many parts of Africa and the East. The latter were brought to the Cape in large numbers by the Dutch East India Company. After the British occupation in 1806 and the establishment of the naval base at Simon's Town in 1814, the British also brought people from their colonies: 'Kroomen' from West Africa, slaves and artisans from Mozambique, Angola, Madagascar, India, Zanzibar, China, Ceylon, St Helena and even Tristan da Cunha. Inevitably, relationships developed between these various groups, which resulted in the colourful, multi-cultural society of the naval port.

The arrival of the British fundamentally changed the nature of Simon's Town. No longer was it purely a place for commercial enterprise as in the days of the Dutch East India Company. The British found that it was strategically situated at the foot of Africa. With the establishment of the Royal Naval Base, Simon's Town became an arm of British 'gunboat' diplomacy. The influx of the navy over the years of British occupation influenced the make-up of the coloured community. The vast majority of coloured surnames in the area are of British origin. Surnames like Craig, Richards, Roberts, Atkins, Terry, Thompson, Higgins and Jenkins bear witness to these roots.

As a naval town, Simon's Town grew rapidly during the latter part of the nineteenth century, when the British Empire was at the height of its power. The southern suburbs railway line finally

A West African 'Krooman' employed by the British Navy, ca. 1888. Many of these seamen later settled in Simon's Town.

(Simon's Town Museum)

reached the town, providing an important transport link to Cape Town. The Dockyard was expanded and Xhosa-speaking people were brought from the Eastern Cape as a labour force. Africans were mainly employed for unskilled and hard labour at the naval base. Originally they were housed in appalling conditions near Seaforth and eventually moved to the Luyolo location site in 1900. They lived on terraces cut into the mountain facing the Naval Dockyards from the north. Conditions in the Luyolo location were very poor. The African community was reduced to living in what was virtually a ghetto. African people were removed from Simon's Town in 1965, two years before the Group Areas proclamation. They were removed by government trucks within two weeks and re-housed in Guguletu. Their story still needs to be told. Was this their punishment for taking part in the march to Jubilee Square and the burning of pass books in 1960 after the massacre at Sharpeville and Langa?[5]

After the Second World War Britain was faced with a huge war debt. The Simon's Town Royal Naval Base became a casualty of the cutbacks. And in 1957 the British handed the base over to South Africa. Some people in Simon's Town felt that they had been abandoned by Britain.[6] They were shocked because Simon's Town was considered British territory and supposedly immune to South Africa's racial laws. As Mr W.K. recalls, 'The main thing was that I was afraid that England would let us down and my fears were confirmed, it was confirmed with the Group Areas.'

Second to the Naval Base in providing employment was the fishing industry. Before removals, line fishing was an important occupation that was almost exclusively carried out by

Luyolo location in the 1920s

(Simon's Town Museum)

Treknet fishing at Cole Point

(Simon's Town Museum)

coloured fisherman. Daily, many fishing boats went out early, weather permitting, and returned with large hauls of fish such as yellowtail and snoek. Treknet fishing was another predominantly coloured fishing activity. The Miller family trekked fish at Froggy Pond, the Jaffa family at Cole Point, the Cotton family at Long Beach, the Breda family at Kleinvishoek, and the Jacobs family at Glencairn. Today, only the Cotton and Aghmat families continue with treknet fishing.[7]

Before the Removals: Community Life in Simon's Town

Memories of life in pre-removals Simon's Town reveal a community where doors were seldom locked and where crime was minimal. My interviewees were mainly born in the 1930s. I heard stories of a generation whose lives were shaped very differently to the lives of later generations. Their parents had memories of experiences of the devastating First World War, the insecure 1920s and the depression years of the 1930s, to be followed by the Second World War.

Over the years, the Naval Dockyard at Simon's Town employed many coloured workers, both skilled and unskilled. In the 1940s, the Second World War provided opportunities for work and skills acquisition. This brought wealth and educational vistas for the workers' children,

The opening of Waterfalls Flats, 1946

(Simon's Town Museum)

The day's catch: yellowtail caught by George Cotton's trek fishermen

(Simon's Town Museum)

A typical kitchen scene

(Simon's Town Museum)

changing coloured citizens' lives completely. Coloured workers were trained by the British to perform highly skilled work, which at that time was reserved for white workers beyond the Dockyard walls.[8]

These experiences played a crucial part in shaping and influencing the coloured community of Simon's Town, such as in the ways in which they raised their children. A strict childhood with an almost Victorian morality was hammered into them. Interviewees said that they learnt their good habits from their parents. 'I never lifted my hand to my wife. When we turned out the lights, everything was over again.' Referring to discipline, Mr K.K. recalled his mother saying, 'I don't bring you up for myself, but for other people, that I should respect others.' Some parents were not as gentle. Mrs M.R. remembered, 'If one did something wrong, we all used to get a hiding with the belt.'

The church played a major part in instilling a strict sense of morality in the community. Churches were regularly overcrowded on Sundays. The Roman Catholic, Anglican and Methodist churches were the most important

Mrs Roseline Kindo and fellow churchgoers Mrs Maria Christians and Mrs Minky Cyster returning home from church down the lane from Cardiff Road on a Sunday morning

(Copyright: George Hallett)

Christian churches in Simon's Town. The Roman Catholic Church was built in 1850 and celebrated its 150th anniversary in 2000. Generally, children were required to attend the morning and evening service and also the Sunday School. 'Our whole life revolved around the churches, because my mother was a very "churchy" person' (Mr A.A.). The annual Sunday School outing was another great occasion. Parents would join their children to spend a day in Red Hill, Witsands, Camel Rock or some other recreation area nearby. Competitive games were played, such as one-legged races, sack races, egg-and-spoon races – to the great delight of everyone.

The church also played an important part in home life. 'We could never go to bed without saying our prayers' (Mr J.D.). Sons and daughters joined the Church Lads Brigade or Girls Brigade of the Anglican Church, where they learnt to play various instruments such as bugles, clarinets, flutes, piccolos and drums. They would practise during the week and march with those who did not play any instruments, from one end of the town to the other. Sunday was their big day and their music would make you creep out of bed guiltily if you had not gone to church that day. The Church Lads Brigade of the Anglican Church has celebrated its 75th anniversary, taking into account the break caused by the removals. One of its members, Mr L.C., became the national head of the organisation, as Commanding Officer of Cape Town's diocesan regiment.[9]

Other recreational activities included camping either at Easter or Christmas time. Places such as Witsands, Schuster's Kraal (Scarborough) and the 'Lawns' near Soetwater were popular. Platboom and Olifantsbos in the Cape Point Nature Reserve were other favourite places. If they ran out of food they would often just catch fish, crayfish or abalone, as Mr R.W. recalled. At that time there were no restrictions on catches or sizes.

According to Ms I.M. there were '[a] lot of parties, family parties, friends' parties, birthday parties and that type of thing'. Almost every Saturday there was a dance in either the Alfred Hall, or the Church Hall, or the Sailors' and Soldiers' Rest Room, or a school hall. There were many places to meet friends to have a 'nice' time (Ms I.M.). Many local bands, like the Blue Gardenias, played regularly at dances and even at white venues like the Glencairn Hotel. Community bands played at weddings and 21st birthday parties (Mr J.D.).

Many of the men of the Anglican and Methodist churches were members of the Free Gardeners, a South African offshoot of the Scottish Lodge. It was the only known Lodge that admitted coloureds, whereas the Freemasons, the Foresters and the Phoenix Lodge did not.[10] The Free Gardeners were a benefit society that provided financial, moral and religious support to its members. It was so popular that it even had a junior section for young boys from 6 to 16. The Simon's Town chapter, known as the Star of Kilmarnock,

Well-known Simon's
Town resident Omar Pott
celebrating his 100th
birthday, ca. 1960

(Simon's Town Museum)

Imam Baker at the Muslim
School in Thomas Street

(Simon's Town Museum)

was wealthy enough to purchase its own hall in the Main Road. It had to sell the hall at the time of the removals.

Most people were poor to very poor; however 'there was nobody who would starve or go begging' (Mr K.K.). Despite the poverty 'there were always food on the table' (Mrs T.F.). Generally, breakfast consisted of a cup of coffee and sandwiches. Lunch was unheard of. Supper was usually a big meal of cooked food, such as a stew or fried fish, to which the whole family would sit down. On Sundays a traditional large lunch was served with lots of meat and vegetables. At Christmas time a huge lunch was shared with visiting relatives 'from up the line' who usually spent a week or two in Simon's Town (Mr S.T.).

Simon's Town's coloured community was generally very literate. Catholics, Anglicans and Muslims had their own schools and one high school reached matriculation level. While there was a municipal library, very few coloureds used it as it was perceived to be a library for whites only. Often a mother or a sister who worked for some madam or other brought home magazines and books. 'My mother got them from the white people' (Mr R.W.). Despite a fair level of education (most Simon's Town people had at least a Standard Six [Grade Eight] pass by 1950) very few indulged in politics, discussed it or dared to join political

organisations. Mr G.T. states, 'No, we weren't politically minded', and Mrs T.F. said, 'Never! Never, nogal'.

There is strong evidence to suggest that Simon's Town was racked by racial, group and class prejudices. Racism was as prevalent in this community as it was throughout the country. 'It was there, but we never used to worry about it ... People created their own apartheid' (Ms I.M.). Skin colour, hair texture and origin acquired an unnatural importance. Some sports clubs did not even accept Muslims as members. Mrs T.F. related that to become members, Muslims had to adopt a Christian surname or a 'football surname'. Class prejudices surfaced on the issue of where someone lived. Certain parts of the town were considered unacceptable, even if relatives were living there. Those who lived in Mount Pleasant considered themselves 'better' than their poorer cousins living in the Kloof in the Council flats.

Contact between the coloured community and the African community of Luyolo was also virtually nil. Although some young coloured people attended the night school in the Luyolo location during the 1950s, few friendships developed between them.

A demeaning manifestation of racism in Simon's Town was the phenomenon of 'play-white-ism'. At that time some coloureds who were fair and long-haired enough would pretend to be white. As in the rest of the country, any number of mixed families consisted of a white and a coloured section. All interviewees were able to rattle off the names of these divided families: the Dubbers, Craigs, Trederees, Burchells and Springhalls. Doubtlessly there were privileges associated with being white, such as a better education, better jobs, and more

Albert Thomas's son and a friend playing soccer in Cardiff Road in front of their homes

(Copyright: George Hallett)

Children in Budge's Lane

(Simon's Town Museum)

opportunities.[11] I remember sitting in the upstairs coloured section of the only cinema in Simon's Town as a young man and being told by a friend, 'You see that white boy sitting down there [in the white section downstairs] – he's my bladdy cousin!' And Mr G.T. advised me that 'I am not ashamed to say so, my sisters also used to sit downstairs, they were fair ... they waited till the picture started'. Mrs J.O. related a sad story about her white relative:

> We had a white uncle that worked as a shoe-maker in Simon's Town. He was a relative of my daddy, but we didn't know it. We weren't supposed to know because he was white. But then I used to pass and go to the butcher and this man, we would sometimes take shoes to him, he would stare at me all the time and I had the feeling that he knew that I was Jasper's [his brother's] child. But he couldn't say that because he was white and we were coloured.

Playing dominoes in Luyolo location, 1964

(Simon's Town Museum)

Luyolo location, 1964

(Simon's Town Museum)

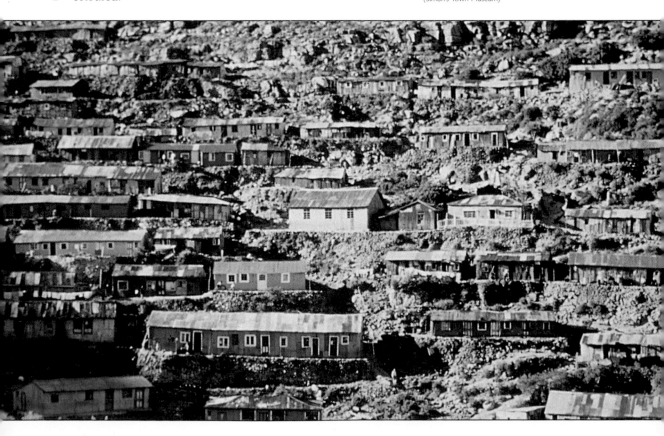

Wedding celebration in Luyolo location, 1964

(Simon's Town Museum)

Before forced removals the coloured people of Simon's Town were generally an active, 'happy-go-lucky' community. People were very involved in family, church, sport and recreation. As 'good' citizens, who lived morally and religiously correct lives, their removal under the Group Areas Act was an event that many could not fathom. The stroke of a bureaucratic pen left them bewildered and betrayed.

Forced Removals and the 1967 Proclamation

Simon's Town's coloured and African people were never a highly politicised community. They never acted jointly in protest against the apartheid regime. Years of informal segregation under the British, followed by apartheid, conditioned all groups at that time. Very few questioned the state of affairs and those who did were regarded with suspicion and, at worst, ostracised. But the proclamation of September 1967, declaring greater Simon's Town a white group area, resulted in the formation of a small protest group opposing the removals. Mr A. Amlay, the son of a coloured municipal councillor, was initially the Chairperson and Mr Roberts, the primary school's principal, was elected Secretary. Mrs Barbara Willis, wife of a Simon's Town historian and active in the Black Sash, later became the Chairperson.

Many meetings were held and petitions drawn up, but as Mr Amlay said, 'We knew that it wasn't going to help ... we knew it was useless ... but we tried to get as much publicity as possible.' This resulted in the security police visiting their homes, with the obvious intention of intimidating them into silence. Unresponsiveness to politics was, therefore, not the only reaction. There was also the feeling of defencelessness in opposing the all-powerful state. As Mrs M.K. said, 'We didn't do anything. We felt we couldn't do anything.' Most of the coloured men worked for the South African Navy and feared dismissals if they participated in any form of political activism.

Fear was certainly a common denominator during those days. Mrs T.F. telephoned me a day after I had interviewed her and asked me to come back, as she felt that there were a few things she wanted to tell me, especially how her husband lost his job in the Dockyard in 1966.

I went from my home, walking down the Main Road unaware of what had taken place in the Dockyard … Thinking about it afterwards I realised why people and friends were giving me meaningful looks and also avoiding me. Later that afternoon William [her husband] arrived but he did not tell me anything despite my asking him why he was home so early. But I could see from the worried look on his face that something had happened. Only the next day could I put the pieces together of what had taken place. William and some workers were in front of an office in the Dockyard when the news of Dr Verwoerd's murder spread like wildfire throughout the Dockyard. He and another person remarked that they would be rejoicing that night as that *vark* [pig] of apartheid should have been killed long ago. A Dockyard official had overheard these remarks and came out demanding to know who had said such bad things about Dr Verwoerd. A.B. told the officer that it was William … who was immediately detained, the police were called in and he was taken to Simon's Town police station where the security police questioned him. He was immediately sacked from the Dockyard without any benefits. It was many years later that A.B. spoke to William and made his peace with him.[12]

There was also some positive reaction from some white citizens who opposed the removals. Mrs I.C., who lived in Seaforth, remembered that

A view of Simon's Town's Main Road, with the old Post Office building in the foreground, ca. 1950

(Simon's Town Museum)

Mrs T.

Mrs T. was born in Simon's Town in 1932. Her family was large; she had four brothers and five sisters. Two had already died when she was born. Like most coloured families she was of mixed parentage and could rattle off all the details. Her one grandfather, a Russian Jew, returned to Russia in the 1920s and never came back. Her other grandfather 'looked like an African'. She told me that one day her mother slapped her eldest sister in the street. A white lady remonstrated that she would report her mother to the police for hitting the madam's child! She remembers going to school barefoot because 'everyone went bare feet as you only got one pair of shoes each year'.

She left school in Standard Five (Grade Seven) and was working in a sweet factory in Woodstock when she was 13 years old. But before that she also did some domestic work, being paid ten shillings (R1,00) for a morning's work. This was supplemented by '*bietjie van die en 'n bietjie van daai van die miesies*' [a little of this and a little of that which the madam gave you].

Mrs T. eventually married. Her husband's father, a naval officer, had left his mother when he returned to Britain. She showed me several love letters that her husband's father had written to his mother.

her white neighbours said, 'What are we going to do with you people? ... We used to live in harmony ... We lived like brothers and sisters.' There were many mixed families who were now separated by the proclamation. When it came to the actual removals, the white section was allowed to remain in Simon's Town while the coloured section had to move to Ocean View or elsewhere. The dilemma was complete. Mrs I.C. quotes a white neighbour as having said, 'You know, I think you people have got more white on your backsides than we have got on ours!'

Public enquiries were held about the feasibility of group areas in Simon's Town as early as August 1959. Various churches and groups from the community set up a liaison committee to make representations at these meetings. There was not a single representative who indicated that group areas were 'wanted or warranted in Simon's Town'.[13]

Soon after the proclamation of 1 September 1967, officials of the Department of Community Development arrived in Simon's Town. They worked closely with the local municipality and the Black Sash liaison committee, which had set up an advice office in the town. It was estimated that between 5 000 and 6 000 coloureds would be moved, over and above the 1 500 African people who had been moved in 1965. The white popula-

tion at that time was estimated at about 3 600, which means that more than 65 per cent of the population was removed.[14]

Government officials arrived in their white Volkswagen Beetles, the favoured government vehicle at that time, and visited all the families to determine their housing needs. The first real movement took place in 1968. Complete evacuation was effected by 1974. Some people did not move to Ocean View. Many landowners were able to purchase fine homes in the coloured suburbs of the southern Peninsula. Many of the artisan class working in the Naval Dockyard qualified for government subsidies and also moved to these areas. They did not wish to live in a township called Slangkop (Snake's Head)![15]

Property owners in Simon's Town were given a cut-off date to sell their property on the open market. If they did not sell by that date the Department of Community Development would purchase the property at a price determined by itself.[16] These prices were not market-related and many people lost money as a result. Mr A.A. disclosed that his family received R29 000 for two shops on Main Road, which are valued at close to a million rands today. The fate of the Indian shopkeeping community was very precarious. Initially it was stated that they would have to move to the only Indian group area in the Peninsula, Rylands

Apartheid signs at the bookstall at Simon's
Town Station, 1967

(Simon's Town Museum)

The front page of the lease agreement between
the author and the old Cape Divisional Council.
He and his family were forcibly removed from
Cardiff Road to 7 Allison Court in Ocean View,
'with effect from 3.7.1970'.

(Source: Albert Thomas)

Estate. It is unclear why they were eventually allowed to remain.

The vast majority of Simon's Town residents were tenants, as very few coloureds owned their own homes.[17] Those who lived in the municipality-owned flats in the Kloof area and the Dido Valley cottages were dependent on government officials' decisions to house them in Ocean View. As housing became available in Ocean View, these officials decided who qualified for a cottage or flat. In exceptional cases, the aged, disabled, or larger families could appeal for alternative accommodation. Thus the aged and disabled could be allocated flats at ground level or cottages.

THE DIVISIONAL COUNCIL OF THE CAPE

Telephone : 41-3266   44 Wale Street,
P.O. Box 1073   (56)   CAPE TOWN.
TB/AEH   .....23/6/70......

Mr./Mrs. A.H. Thomas...   24/2/79 - to 3 Zodiac Road,
..."Hilson"...   Ocean View
...Cardiff Road...
...Simonstown.

Dear Sir/Madam,

4R/E   OCEAN VIEW HOUSING SCHEME

        With reference to your application for a letting in the
abovementioned scheme, I wish to advise you that it is found
possible to allocate letting No. ...7 Allison Court.....,
Ocean View to you, with effect from ......3.7.70...........

        If you are prepared to accept the abovementioned letting,
it will be necessary for you to call at the office situated at the
scheme at Ocean View at 10-00 AM. on .....3.7.70...........
to sign the necessary Agreement of Lease and to make a payment of
R 21.-..67 being one month's rent.

        Please complete and return the undermentioned form to
me as soon as possible in regard to this allocation.

                                Yours faithfully,

                        for G. S. MALAN
                             SECRETARY

I, ...Albert Thomas...
acknowledge receipt of the abovementioned allocation and would
advise that I am/am not prepared to accept the allocation offered.

        I declare that if I am not prepared to accept this allo-
cation, I will, myself, find alternative accommodation for my family
and declare further, that I do not hold the Department of Community
Development or any other Authority responsible for finding alternative accommodation.

        I undertake to move from my present accommodation as soon
as a removal notice has been served on me.
Date : ...24/6/70......   A.Thomas..........
                                    (Signature)
Witnesses:
1. ....
2. ....

A copy of the rent card issued to the author by the Department of Community Development. He was subsequently liable to pay the Department rent until he was moved to Ocean View in 1970. The card had to be produced when making rent payments.

(Source: Albert Thomas)

Larger families could qualify for three-bedroom semi-detached cottages, depending on availability.

For the first time families were divided into three types of housing: economic, sub-economic and self-help. Economic accommodation provided hot water cylinders, doors to each room and baths in the bathrooms. These extras were not fitted in sub-economic houses and flats. Economic and sub-economic housing consisted of one- or two-bedroom flats in three-storey blocks of flats occupied by twelve families. Semi-detached cottages consisting of two bedrooms (and a limited number consisting of three bedrooms) were also built. Later, single- and double-storey maisonettes were built for the economic group. Eventually three areas of free-standing two- and three-bedroom houses for homeowners from the self-help group were built.

Rents payable were not to exceed 25 per cent of a family's income. No lodgers or boarders were allowed without permission or a written permit from the Community Development Board. No accommodation was provided for single people. The Simon's Town municipality provided free transport of household goods to those families who occupied municipal flats or cottages. Those living in private accommodation had to provide their own transport to move their furniture and goods to Ocean View or elsewhere.[18]

In many cases, rents in Simon's Town were cheaper because the houses were older. As the people were moved out of their homes in Simon's Town their houses were demolished, although most of these were still perfectly liveable. The first 40 families were moved to the sub-economic houses at the end of August 1968 and 28 families were moved to the economic houses at the end of October. Thereafter, 75 per cent of housing that became available went to Simon's Town families. The balance went to families from Noordhoek and other Divisional Council areas that had also been declared white.[19]

Some people tried to delay their removal for as long as possible. Mr A.A. recalled that the Department of Community Development had to get a senior naval officer to persuade him to move. He was then presented with an ultimatum from the Dockyard, as it had purchased the family home. This finally forced his hand. Mr G.T. told me that officials eventually arrived with the sheriff and some labourers. They physically removed all his furniture and goods and placed it in the sandy garden in front of his home. They then proceeded to board up the home in which he was born, married and had lived in for sixty years.

Ocean View: Problems with Settling in

Immediately after the forced move, many people experienced feelings of alienation and displacement. They needed time to come to terms with a place that was strange and unfamiliar. No longer were the familiar landmarks of False Bay and the high Simonsberg mountains in sight. They had to discover where friends and relatives were living. It was a case of new neighbours in new surroundings that still had to be absorbed. Some settled in easily, like Mrs M.R.: 'Mind you, after a few weeks we got used to it.' But Mr R.W., who was moved from the Seaforth area, complained bitterly. 'I felt lost. I really thought to myself, how are we going to survive in this place?'

People also encountered many practical problems. The immediate difficulty was the lack of transport. At the beginning, in 1968, most people who did not have their own vehicles were forced to walk to Fish Hoek, a distance of ten kilometres. Mr J.D. remembers the frustration and inconvenience that this caused in his home: 'Father was a fisherman and had to be in Simon's Town between 4.00 a.m. and 5.00 a.m. My dad used to take the last one! [the last bus the previous night] ...

Sometimes he would get a lift from somebody, but if he missed the lift, he had it! Then they just had to stay at home. There was no other transport.'

The South African Navy sent trucks to Ocean View for their workers and took them back each day after work. Later, as the removals increased, a more regular bus service was arranged to Fish Hoek and Simon's Town. Much later, the kombi-taxi service arrived. Today, both the kombi-taxi services cease operating after 8.30 p.m. Most people therefore become prisoners of this township if they do not possess their own transport.

In the beginning there were no schools or churches. Schools in Simon's Town arranged buses to take their pupils back to their homes in the afternoons. Mrs I.C., who was one of the first to be moved, informed me that her children had to take a bus to Simon's Town. 'All three of my children were at the Catholic School at that time. Then from there, when the school opened here, which was three to four years after that, then they were transferred to this school over here.' Currently there are two primary schools (one English-medium and the other Afrikaans-medium) and a high school to matriculation level.

Church services were held in people's homes, while others travelled back to Simon's Town until

Mrs I.

Mrs I. was born in 1926 in Seaforth, Simon's Town, and lived there all her life before she was moved to Ocean View in 1968. Her family was among the first to be moved there. She had three brothers and three sisters. Her one grandfather was a Filipino, the other came from Scotland. One of her grandmothers came from Ireland. Her father died three weeks before she had to move to Ocean View.

She first went to the Girls Mission School (opposite the Simon's Town clock), and thereafter to the Corpus Christi School in Heathfield. All her brothers went to the Catholic School and were taught by the nuns. She obtained her Standard Eight (Grade Ten) certificate and studied nursing for three years. Because her mother was bedrid-

den with severe asthma, she was forced to look after her for many years. She remembers having to cook food for the family from a very early age, and that her brothers and sisters had to fetch wood in the mountains for the fire.

Mrs I.'s grandmother was a midwife and she often accompanied her by horse cart all over the town and beyond. She remembers going with her grandmother to deliver babies for the farm workers at Imhoff's Farm, where present-day Ocean View is situated. She recalls details of the farm, and the many fruit trees and vegetables that were cultivated there. Mr van der Horst, the owner of Imhoff's Farm, always had his rifle with him and he had a long beard. Little did she know that many years later she would be living there.

churches were built in Ocean View. There are currently churches for the seven major Christian denominations, as well as a mosque. Various charismatic Christian groups also hold services in all the schools. Four shops were built: a butcher, café, fish-and-chips shop, and a general dealer's shop, which opened only at the end of 1968. Prior to this, the first residents had to purchase all their goods in either Fish Hoek or Simon's Town and carry them all the way to Ocean View. Only much later was a supermarket built to provide a more comprehensive variety of provisions and goods.

The youth in particular found themselves dislocated. It took many years before the churches or authorities built community halls, a sports field, a cinema and a bar/lounge where dances and discos were held. Mrs J.O. often told her children about Simon's Town.

> I tell my children about Simon's Town; swimming, the mountain! You know what my children tell me? And you brought us up in this hole! They can't understand that I had such a happy childhood. Here they can't go anywhere. There is nothing for them ... They don't like Ocean View ... They don't even have friends, their family is their friends.

Problems also arose between the youth from Simon's Town and Noordhoek. Noordhoek–Sunnydale was also declared a white group area and coloureds from there were settled in Ocean View. The Noordhoek community was considered by some to be rural, Afrikaans-speaking, less educated and unsophisticated. By contrast, the Simon's Town community generally considered itself to be English-speaking, suburban and better educated. Clashes were inevitable, especially over weekends, and the mixture of liquor and discos led to physical encounters and even murder. Names were invented for the gangs who were responsible for these incidents: the 'Noordhoekers' and the 'Simonites'. The problem only disappeared when intermarriage between the youth of these two groups eventually diluted their differences.

Ocean View is still essentially a township where people eat and sleep, and live very constrained lives. Those who are employed have to go to their places of employment daily and return at night after work. In the new, less spacious homes, furniture was often too large and had to be broken up. In some cases people discovered that it was impossible to move furniture up the narrow stairs of blocks of flats or small maisonettes allocated to them. Mr B.L. recalled, 'People had to give a lot of their furniture away because they couldn't get it in. Although we lived in wood-and-iron shacks in Glencairn, people had decent furniture.'

Those living in flats and maisonettes were not

Mr J.

Mr J. was born in 1930 in Kleinvishoek, where the Marine Oil refinery is in Glencairn. His father was a fisherman, trekking fish on the beach opposite the refinery. He was told that his great-grandfather came from Peru and started whaling in False Bay towards the end of the nineteenth century. His great-grandfather, grandfather and father all had the same first name. Mr J. said that his grandfather could still speak Spanish and died when he was 97 years old. They were poor, but managed to get a basic education at the Catholic School.

He had to leave school after passing Standard Five (Grade Seven) to help his family. He had seven brothers and three sisters. As a young man he helped his father trek fish. He did a lot of diving to check that the fishnets did not get snagged on the many wrecks around Kleinvishoek. The Royal Navy, especially during the war years, often practised firing its guns from the gun battery across the road where they lived. When this happened, they had to go and sit at Glencairn Station and on their return they had to search for their livestock. 'The chickens used to disappear for days,' the dog had to be pulled from under the bed and the broken crockery had to be picked up from the floor. Growing up in Kleinvishoek was tough for them.

allowed to keep pets. Mrs L. from Welcome Farm in Glencairn recalled how the Animal Welfare arrived before their removal to Ocean View to put down their animals, which were then buried in a large prepared grave. She said it was a terrible sight, with children and adults wailing over the death of their pets.[20] Many of the people from the outlying areas such as Red Hill and Glencairn also had chickens, ducks and other farm animals, or they cultivated large gardens of vegetables and flowers. These activities were no longer possible for residents who were allocated either flats or maisonettes.

Social life and family life were severely disrupted. It took many years to repair this as families were separated, not only from those who were classified white, but also because many moved to areas on the Cape Flats. Some even emigrated overseas and saw their families only after the unbanning of political organisations in 1990.

The Impact of the Removals

There is no doubt that the removals had severe negative psychological effects, especially on older people. Mr B.W. informed me that when he dreams, 'I always dream of Simon's Town. I never dream about Ocean View'. Many other interviewees confirmed that the location of their dreams was Simon's Town, indicating the unconscious sense of place and landscape that Simon's Town held. But the children and youth appeared to have settled in Ocean View much more easily. 'I must say they all settled in well!' (Mrs M.R.). Mr A.A. remarked, 'It changed everybody's lives', both black and white.

For some people the move was not entirely unfavourable. Those who lived in the informal settlement at Welcome Farm in Glencairn or Red Hill, where there was no electricity and a lack of other services, found the move advantageous. For the first time many of them had homes with inside flush toilets, electricity, hot and cold water and refuse removals. For people such as Mrs M.K. standards of living improved considerably after the move. But despite these positive aspects, she still missed the natural surroundings of her former home:

There in Red Hill, when you used to open your front door, you could look into the Dockyard and all that down to Simon's Town. There if you open your door you look into the mountains. Here if you open your door you look into other peoples' houses, in the front and the back! I just can't get used to that, and in Red Hill it was also a lot safer.

Ocean View Township

(Simon's Town Museum)

The older generation still speaks nostalgically about Simon's Town. Some even believe that Simon's Town was a paradise. In answer to my question whether this was so, 72-year-old Mr S.R. replied, 'A paradise? I wouldn't say it was a paradise, but it was a nice place to stay in, it was safe!' Most interviewees acknowledged that the 'good old days' were gone forever and had no wish to go back to Simon's Town now that the group areas had been abolished. At their age they did not want to start all over again. Others have established roots and settled down. Family and friends, schools and churches, sports organisations and other infrastructures are in Ocean View. To move back to Simon's Town would just create another upheaval in their lives.

The establishment of the ghetto of Ocean View by the Group Areas Act succeeded to such a degree that most of its people would find it very difficult to return to Simon's Town. The cost of land and housing there is now beyond the reach of most of them. Older people are dying and the younger ones have little knowledge of or allegiance to the naval town. But there are others who feel strongly about the terrible injustice that has been done and insist that some form of return or restitution should take place. Mr W.K. indicated that he was prepared to erect a shack on his family's land, that nothing would stop him from regaining the land held by his family since 1862.

On the question of forgiveness, Mr A.A.'s comment echoed most of the interviewees' feelings. 'The Lord can forgive us, why can't we forgive? But forget? You can't! You can never forget!' Mr W.K. spoke of an unresolved anguish and anger that comes from the heart of a committed Christian who has struggled deeply with the outrage he has suffered.

> I tell you ... to me an injustice has been done and I never really came to terms with it. I told the priest also. It is hard for me to take communion and all that. If I went on my own, I would have accepted it. But to be chased out of my home because of my colour, that is one thing I will fight unto my death, that part of it! Unfortunately that has wasted

> a lot of my life, it never really made me accept this place as home.

Memory and Identity in Ocean View

These interviews indicate that the impact of forced removals on Simon's Town's coloured community left few people untouched. It was not only the physical separation of families, but as Field explains, '[l]osing a home and a community is about a loss of security, stability, autonomy and even a sense of family, friendships and self'.[21]

Mr J.D., who had obviously wrestled with the problem of identity before the removals, now states, 'One thing that could be a good thing is your personality. You knew [now] who you were. Finally you are a coloured and you stay amongst coloured people and the whites stay where they are.' For this man the group areas removals succeeded in their intention of residential separation of the various groups and he confirms how insidious this ideology was.

But many others have not accepted such a simple resolution of the difficult question of coloured identity. Many still have problems even with the word 'coloured' itself and reject it. Goldin argues that this identity problem has been deliberately created by successive white governments. 'For over a century attempts have been made to foster and manipulate this identity and to engineer socially a Coloured political alliance with the ruling White parties.'[22] The National Party especially attempted to 'promote a distinct Coloured identity in South Africa' with the formation of the Tricameral Parliament. But the election results of 1994 paint another picture.[23]

What these academic analyses seem to ignore are the basic elements of identity.[24] Identity is also created by memories of togetherness at home, in the street and in the neighbourhood. This sense of belonging and shared memory patterns are also powerful elements of identity. So what is the 'problem of identity' then for people formerly classified as coloured? I wish to suggest that the vast majority certainly do not reject themselves as human beings. In my view, most coloured people, especially those who live in the numerous township ghettoes, do not have an identity crisis. They are too occupied with the day-to-day struggle of managing their lives and the usual problems that accompany this struggle.

Conclusion

These stories I listened to have filled me with a sense of my own loss as someone who has also experienced forced removal. They have brought back unpleasant memories of a time when feelings of helplessness and hopelessness pervaded those dark days of the 1960s. After the massacres of Sharpeville and Langa, the all-powerful apartheid state used an iron fist to suppress all opposition.

This may very well explain why the state was able to enforce not only the group areas removals, but also to neutralise a seemingly submissive people with an array of repressive legislation.

The vast majority of Ocean View people would find it difficult to return to Simon's Town. But a few who could afford it, have returned. Those who remain have formed a development organisation, its stated purpose being to initiate a large-scale return to Simon's Town, for them and their descendants. They are demanding from the South African Navy and the Commission on Restitution of Land Rights the return of land and buildings. Soon Simon's Town's streets will once again resound with the voices of people of colour who were so callously herded from their homes more than thirty years ago.[25]

Mr W.

Mr W. was born in 1923 in Cardiff Road, Simon's Town. He told me that he was born in the same bedroom as his father, as the family had owned the home since 1862.

William related the story of his great-grandfather, which has been handed down through three or four generations. His great-grandfather was a slave who was thrown overboard when the slave ship he was travelling on was apprehended by a British naval boat off the coast of West Africa. He was fished out of the water and brought to Simon's Town by the Reverend Barnabas Shaw, the founder of the Methodist Church in South Africa. He grew up in the church grounds and was later given land to farm in the area of Goede Gift. Later the family moved to Cardiff Road and lived in their own double-storey home until they were forcibly removed.

Mr W. moved to Grassy Park in 1970. He had two brothers and two sisters. His father worked in the Naval Dockyard for fifty years. His mother came from Cape Town and her family was originally from St Helena. Mr W. left school in Standard Five (Grade Seven) and worked in several places before settling down with the Simon's Town municipality where he worked for more than twenty-eight years. His father was very strict and had 'half a dozen canes' to discipline them with. But the family was very close and all social and religious activities were led by his parents. There may have been strict discipline as they grew up, but there was also a rapport between parents and children, which they appreciated.

7 | 'Mense van die Vlak': Community and Forced Removals in Lower Claremont

Felicity Swanson

For many, a community is not simply the place where we live. It is much more than that – the community is our home. It is the place where many of us were born and it is the place where we will die. It is the place we come home to after a heavy day's work to rest, to be with our friends and neighbours. It is a place of warmth, of friendship, of neighbourly quarrels. Even though our lives may be hard our community gives us strength and hope.[1]

When lower Claremont was declared a white area under the Group Areas Act in November 1969, it was a densely populated area and home to a dynamic community of over 19 000 people.[2] It was a culturally mixed area, comprising coloured, black, white and Indian residents, but the majority was coloured. This community of old or lower Claremont, as most residents called it, had over a long period of time forged a strong sense of identity and community spirit that cut across religious, racial and class divides.

Tucked below the railway line, lower Claremont formed one of three pockets of mixed

Claremont Station, ca. 1890

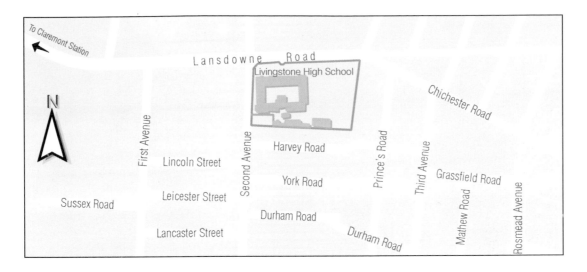

areas sandwiched in by the broader white residential suburb of Claremont. Widely known as *die Vlak* (the Flats), the area was marked by well-defined physical boundaries, with Bell Road running from Harfield Station, Rosmead Avenue and Chichester Road into Lansdowne Road and back into First Avenue. Lower Claremont was a popular area, because it was near to a network of cheap buses and trains providing easy access to work. It had a self-sufficient infrastructure of over forty shops and small businesses. Some shops had been established for over sixty years and remained successful family businesses.[3] In addition, the community had more than ten schools, including the prestigious Livingstone High School.

Lansdowne Road Hotel and Bottlestore

(University of Cape Town Libraries/Manuscripts and Archives)

View of Claremont Main Road

(University of Cape Town Libraries/Manuscripts and Archives)

The community of lower Claremont no longer exists. During the 1970s and 1980s residents were forced out of their neighbourhood to make way for white development.[4] Today, the area has been transformed into an upmarket residential suburb, known as Harfield Village, with renovated Chelsea cottages and houses, but we hope that the personal memories of the individuals who lived there will reflect the history of this once vibrant community, while demonstrating the emotional costs of dislocation and displacement.

Historical Background: From the Cape Flats to City Suburb

The origins of lower Claremont can be traced back to the late nineteenth century, when the area was part of expanding urban Cape Town. Before the extension of the railway line to Wynberg in 1864, lower Claremont was part of the Cape Flats. It was a poorly developed rural area, flat and sandy, with a few farms dotted around. In winter, large lakes formed

The general dealer, Mr Ali, in First Avenue

(Photograph: Don Pinnock)

and farmers' carts were often stuck in the mud.[5] When Harfield Road Station was built as part of the new southern suburbs line, a number of cottages sprang up in the vicinity. The area continued to grow and in 1883 it was incorporated into the newly formed Liesbeeck municipality along with upper Claremont, Newlands, Rondebosch, Wynberg and Mowbray.[6]

A wedding at St Matthew's Church in Second Avenue

(Photograph: Don Pinnock)

Semi-detached houses in Norfolk Street before removals

(Photograph: Don Pinnock)

By 1889, Saint Saviour's Church in upper Claremont had established a small school and chapel on *die Vlak* to minister to the needs of some one hundred and eighty coloured people living in the area.[7] Many of these people had gradually moved down from the Kirstenbosch and Protea Road areas. Claremont Main Road was also developing rapidly as a commercial centre, attracting more people into the area.[8] In 1890 the entire Claremont area above and below the railway line was granted its own separate municipal status, finally becoming a suburb of greater Cape Town in 1913.[9]

Certainly by the 1960s lower Claremont was a well-established area. Three main avenues – First, Second and Third – ran parallel to each other, with all the streets branching off them. All the streets had English names, such as Surrey, Durham, Lancaster, York and Leicester, reflecting earlier connections to a British cultural heritage. These remain to the present day, although the area was renamed Harfield Village after it was declared white and transformed by the forced removals of the 1970s and 1980s. The roads of the housing development in Sherwood Park in Philippi, where some Claremont residents moved, were all given the same names.[10]

There were a number of well-established churches in the area. St Matthew's Anglican Church and the Methodist Church were both in Second Avenue, St Ignatius Catholic Church in Lansdowne Road and the Dutch Reformed Church in Durham Street, where the Zionists held services every Saturday afternoon. Mrs A.W., a resident of some fifty years, recalls the distinctive black, red and white colours of the uniforms of female members of the Methodist Church and remembers the popular meaning of those colours: 'If your sins are as black as my stockings and they wash in the blood of my red cloak they will become as white as snow, as my hat that I have got on.' The Harvey Road Mosque served the large Muslim community, but residents could also attend services in the nearby Stegman Road Mosque and the mosque in Main Road, Claremont. For Christian and Muslim communities, the church and the mosque were the focus of both their spiritual and social lives.

People chatting on the corner of Second Avenue and Lincoln Street

A backyard scene

Children playing in Wesley Street

(Photographs: Don Pinnock)

Social Life in Lower Claremont before 1970

The community was made up of people from all walks of life and included professional people such as lawyers, doctors and teachers, as well as tradesmen, artisans, Council workers, factory workers, domestic workers, dressmakers, house-wives and hawkers. The majority of people belonged to the working class. Mr S.A. recalled that people who lived above the railway line in the more affluent mixed area of upper Claremont around Draper, Protea and Vineyard Roads, looked down on the Claremont community 'below' the railway line. There was always some competition between these two communities. People from upper Claremont regarded themselves a step above everyone else and liked to joke, '*Haai julle mense van die Vlak, julle is rou*' [Hey, you people from the Flats, you are unrefined]. In a similar fashion, residents of lower Claremont regarded themselves as being better off than the third mixed area below Rosmead Avenue, which was a very poor area and was often referred to as *die Kas* or the Ghost Town.

A few families owned their own houses, but many others rented accommodation. Living conditions in lower Claremont 'were not all that salubrious among poorer people and there was lots of overcrowding' (Mrs A.W.). Housing was scarce and expensive, so two or three families would share one house, which was usually a small semi-detached cottage with a corrugated iron roof. The Langry in Durham Street, a long row of terraced houses, was typical of this and many residents regarded it as a slum area. Families cooked, washed, dressed and ate in one room. Houses were poorly constructed from clay bricks, and had no electricity supply or outside toilets. Landlords were reluctant to make any improvements and tenants struggled to get by in the wet Cape winter. In order to supplement their incomes, many tenants sublet their backyards and allowed people to erect wood and iron shacks. One interviewee remembers how she and her mother lived in such a place when she was a young child. Although conditions were difficult, they still managed to make it a cosy home. But for her, Claremont was 'definitely not heaven, in fact Claremont was a bit of a slum' (Mrs V.D.). These kinds of living conditions later attracted the notice of the National Party, who used these to justify removals under the guise of cleaning up slum areas.

Despite the poverty and generally poor living conditions, lower Claremont was an energetic place, where neighbourliness and community spirit seem to have been valued by people above all else. According to Mrs G.B., 'we all mixed together, coloureds, whites, blacks, Christian and Muslim'. Mr A.C. seems to speak for most people when he comments that Claremont people were poor but respectable, 'a very homely type of people, a close-knit community living a very down-to-earth life with one common ideal: to live together happily'. Mrs G.A. echoes these sentiments: 'We stayed together like a family, like a very close family. We grew up in front of these people and they recognised us, like one of their own, you know and even today when we meet then we are so glad.' Mr A.H., who moved into lower Claremont in the early 1960s after being evicted from Brooklyn when it was declared a white area, recalls the friendliness shown to his family as newcomers to the area. Many families maintained close ties with each other. It was common for relations to live close together, either next door or across the road or around the corner. Mrs R.H.'s grandparents, parents, siblings, aunts and uncles all lived around Second Avenue.

Most ex-residents cherished memories of the Claremont people as being warm and generous.

The entrance to Pop's shebeen

(Photograph: Don Pinnock)

Extended family support networks and general neighbourliness characterised this community before the forced removals of the 1970s and 1980s. Mrs J.G. had several small children to look after while running a busy corner café. Neighbours would willingly come in and sometimes take the children to spend an afternoon in the Claremont Gardens above the Main Road. Mrs G.A. remembers the generosity of neighbours who took her mother to the nursing home by car when she unexpectedly started going into labour. If neighbours were struggling to make ends meet, people would share food generously. Mr A.H. misses the closeness of those times when people were not afraid to ask, 'Hey! What's wrong, is there anything we can do to help?' These family and neighbourhood networks were an important part of community formation and cohesion in Claremont.

Second Avenue was the centre of street life in lower Claremont. Besides being a residential area, Second Avenue also had many small shops. These included grocery, fish, dairy and butcher shops, a bakery, as well as tailors and shoemakers. Someone operated a fish-smoking factory from the backyard of one of these shops. Second Avenue teemed with shoppers and hawkers selling their vegetables from their carts.[11] Many residents did not have regular employment and money was often scarce. They were able to buy 'on tick' (credit) from many shops because they were well known to the owners. They were also able to buy small quantities as few people had fridges.

Mrs R.H. describes Claremont as a rowdy, hectic place. 'We always used to see some drama and did not need to go to the theatre. We used to get it regularly right outside our door.' Boys and girls played street games such as cricket, marbles, spin the top, hide and seek, *drie blikkies* and skipping. During the long summer months games would continue well into the night. Few people owned cars in those days and traffic was light. A man nicknamed 'Ice-blocks' would sell milk ice lollies made by his mom at two for a penny. Mr Davidson sold firecrackers, peanuts and Christmas cards. Mrs Williams sold delicious *vetkoek* and samoosas. Her own mother sold home bakes and people were always popping in to pick up orders. The brothel down the road attracted many foreign sailors and as a child she was spoilt by the 'girls' with sweets and cooldrinks.

Mrs V.D. loved being a child in Claremont. She and her cousins would sit on the pavement like 'birds on a wire' making *seepsop* (bubble soap). She remembers the warmth of the sun on the pavement and the sense of comfort and freedom.

Musician playing at Pop's shebeen

(Photograph: Don Pinnock)

This was my street, where I belonged. People constantly dropping in to Pop's shebeen, our next-door neighbour, always keeping a friendly eye on me, the corners where everyone stopped to chat, the loud arguments between two neighbours that the whole street could hear. The place was a hive of activity from morning to night. People riding up and down, green carts [vegetables], fishmongers, the wood cart, it was like a moving flea market.

Weddings, too, were very much a community affair. There was a great deal of intermarriage as young people in the area met at the local school or started chatting to each other on street corners, further cementing the already strong social bonds. Family, friends and neighbours were invited and all became involved with the preparations. Dressed up in their best outfits, people streamed down the road 'like a lot of ants' carrying chairs, tablecloths and bowls of food. Mrs V.D. could never be bored in Claremont, it was such a fascinating place that was constantly changing. Mrs M.N. remembers the weddings, too. No one was excluded from the celebrations, whether Muslim or Christian. Guests would contribute a plate of eats, keeping the costs down, and the party would spill out into the surrounding streets. Living in Claremont taught her a fundamental lesson in life. 'The main thing in relationships is how people must live with other people, you must tolerate, you must love and hold onto family values.'

Over Christmas and New Year, and during Eid celebrations, the streets were especially exciting. Second Avenue in particular was transformed over the festive season. Street poles were decorated with flowers and Christmas bands and church choirs played and sang in the streets. It was open house for the community. The New Year Street Carnival was a major event for the community. Mr A.S. remembers the hard work and long hours he spent as a member of a troupe:

If you go down Durham Avenue towards Second Avenue, the bottom end, off Durham Avenue on the bend there used to be a row of houses like Chelsea cottages you know, high *stoep* and all that. Now, behind there, that's where we used to start singing, keep our ... every Sunday, Sundays ... sometimes during the week. We had to practise twice or three times a week, Tuesday or whatever because, don't forget we also had to go to the bioscope. So we can't go to the bioscope on singing nights because we got to practise.

Each major street in lower Claremont had its own coon troupe and New Year would bring the coons down Second Avenue. Scores of people would sit outside waiting for the 'Coronations' from the Langry, the 'Happys', the 'Claremont Canadians' and the 'Dixie Boys' in their brightly coloured uniforms to sing and swing down the avenue with hordes of children following their heroes. For many this annual event was eagerly awaited, so much a part of their cultural heritage.

Carnival troupes parade down Second Avenue

(Photograph: Don Pinnock)

Mrs M.H.

Mrs M.H. was born in lower Claremont in 1930 and lived in Third Avenue for over forty-five years. Her father ran a horse-racing stable there. One of her chores as a child was to clean out the stable, which she found hard work. She learnt how to ride at a very young age and helped her father with the training of the horses. Her childhood was quite carefree. Money was never a problem as her father had a good income, both from the stables and from betting at the horse races. People would come to the house on a Friday night to get tips for the races. Every morning at 4 a.m. the stable hands would ride the horses down to Muizenberg beach to exercise. Her mother would have pots full of maize meal dripping with cinnamon and butter ready for them when they returned. Mr Smallberg ran his blacksmith business in the yard. Her mother and father loved to entertain and often held 'hops' in the yard, with everyone dancing till late.

Mrs M.H. was married when she was 15 years old. Although she remembers that as a child no one worried about the colour bar and everyone played together, certain colour restrictions were already in place well before 1948. As a coloured man, her father could not race any horses under his own name, so he had to use the name of a white friend. Her two brothers both became jockeys but could not race in South Africa because of the colour bar. Both went on to ride in Rhodesia. It was an unwritten rule that at the Sunday morning church service at St Saviours, whites sat in the front and coloureds near the back. A number of African families who lived behind the stables in Princess Street ran shebeens. Mrs M.H. recalls with some amusement: 'The Africans, they were very nice the whole week, we would play with their children and everything. But Friday nights! Always fighting on Friday nights! Fight with spades, anything. People were all on their nerves. They did not know what to expect. We all stood ready with our little bundles to run in case they came into our home. We children would run and jump into my uncle's car, an olden time car with no top, and hide.'

We didn't go with knives and guns and pangas to go make enjoyment. I mean we used to go to Hartleyvale, Athlone Stadium, Green Point track, we didn't ride a lorry to our destination, we would walk. From Green Point, walk from Mowbray to Claremont to come and show the people our gear, because the road is all ... the colours of the coons that's in First Avenue, the colour of coons in Second Avenue ... otherwise it's just not New Year. (Mr A.S.)

The New Year Street Carnival raised important class, religious and ethical issues in the community. Not everyone saw the carnival in a positive light. Most coons were hawkers and the coon carnival gave these poorer people a chance to earn money over the holidays by taking collections during the processions. But according to Mr A.H. the coons did everyone a disservice. At a time of intense oppression, their singing, dancing and frivolity in the streets sent out completely the wrong impression and undermined the struggle. Other residents expressed similar sentiments.

I never made any particular effort to watch. Going on like an animal, jumping about like a showpiece, for other people. But being used by the government as a draw card at the end of the year for tourism. All that jumping around in the road is not becoming to a Muslim. If he takes all that uniform money, all those years and put it away, now when the time comes for the child's education, he hasn't got the money. It is all used up for satins and the child is suffering. People overseas don't see the hardships because they look so happy. (Mrs M.N.)

Mr A.S. acknowledges that not all his family supported him while he was a member of the coons. But on a personal level, the coons did provide him with new opportunities.

Ja [yes], couldn't take us being in the coons. Her mother's idea coons is *skollies* [hooligans], you know and yet when coons come down the road they all stand on the *stoep* [verandah] watching the *skollies* you know. So they were all double standards, they were all living double standards that's what I always tell them. Whenever I walk up in Harfield, I always tell them. 'You people were condemning us' and meantime when we came down the road [claps] you all cheer us on, you know, that type of thing. But the coons was a fantastic thing that you could meet new people, learn new things, you know like new songs.

Music was a vital part of Claremont's cultural and social life. Sunday afternoon jazz sessions were held in Mr M.'s house in Princess Square. It was *the* place in the 1950s, drawing patrons from all over the Peninsula to hear the Matewane brothers, Joseph and Stanley, play blues, to dance and generally to relax and have a good time. Patrons would sit around the piano on chairs or on paraffin tins and put money in a saucer when they wanted to request a number. The jive, the kwela, the quickstep and the waltz were popular. One could buy a bottle of sweet wine or brandy from the shebeen in the next room, sit down, relax and have an enjoyable time (Mr A.C.). Mr D.M. led the Princess Square Swingsters, an African musical group started by his brother in the 1940s. After he was forced to move he managed to resuscitate the choir in Nyanga with some of the original Claremont members. 'In 1959 we started getting moved out of Claremont. It changed the whole pattern of the choir. It was difficult to keep the old crowd together because all the people were scattered around' (Mr D.M.).

Mr W.R. organised the Swifts dance club at his mother's house in Durham Street. It was also called the 'tickey bop' club because it was so cheap – twenty cents membership fee, twenty cents for a dance. Through fundraising, by selling curry and rice and drinks from the bar in the kitchen or backyard, and holding Saturday night dances, the group was able to buy a gramophone and records. With entrepreneurial spirit, they then hired themselves out for various dances and functions in the local town hall. Mr A.C. also recalled the raucous parties at the Swifts club. 'Rock and roll on a Saturday night, everyone having a good

Mr D.M.

Mr D.M. was born in Seymour in the Eastern Cape in 1935. He came to live with his brother in Rutland Street in Claremont in 1951 and attended Langa High School. Accommodation was extremely difficult to find. There was only one African township and housing there was very scarce. Claremont was a very convenient area. When Mr D.M. was looking for work it was easy to walk to Wynberg, Claremont, Mowbray and even to town, and he was able to find employment this way. He left school after completing Standard Eight (Grade Ten) and then worked as a shop assistant in Salt River before moving to a men's outfitter in Wynberg, where he worked for thirty-five years.

Mr D.M. spent his leisure time organising the Princess Square Choir, which his brother had started in 1948. After he was forced to move to Guguletu in 1958, he managed to get the choir going again. He also enjoyed going to the cinema and there were several in the area, the Orpheum, the Scala and the Broadway. For Mr D.M. the move to the township was a devastating blow, as he was miles away from anywhere and there was nothing but bush.

After he married he applied to the Langa housing board for a house. But instead of being helped he was harassed by officials who told him that his wife was in Cape Town illegally and that she would have to return to Mdantsane in the Eastern Cape, despite the fact that she had grown up in Retreat. Mr D.M. also said, 'We were given so many names by the apartheid regime. Without debating a bit, these days if you sit down and think about our tax money being spent on changing names, because if you remember we were Kaffirs and Xhosas, then Natives, then Bantus, then Africans, then plurals! All these names you know, reflecting on one group.'

time, jovial and happy. They were the best years of my life.'

Crime and Violence in Lower Claremont

Claremont residents felt that their area was a relatively safe one in comparison to the 'terror-ridden' Cape Flats townships of the 1990s. Although there were a number of gangsters or *skollies* in Claremont, by today's standards they did not cause too much trouble within the community. On a Friday and Saturday night drunken gangs such as the Spoilers and the Billiard Room Gang would gamble and fight on street corners; usually they had fist fights that would break up as soon as the police arrived.

> We had a gang in First Avenue, the Spoilers, in Second Avenue it was the Jungles and then we used to get this one place in Princess Square, that's where the blacks

came. And they would come up, come and fight with the Spoilers, but then we know about it and we would be on our rooftops behind the chimneys with our bottles and our stuff, not guns. They would come with their ... and their *knobkerries* [wooden sticks], I'm telling you. (Mr A.S.)

Lower Claremont was a fairly stable community and as most residents knew each other, the gangs did not pose a threat.

> I mean I used to stay in Harfield, First Avenue, for twenty-eight years, the far end just before Bell Road, next to the 'Ali' Shop – second house next to him for twenty-eight years. That's where I stayed. What about other people? My old man was staying there for fifty years so everyone knew each other and that's why there was no stealing or mugging. We used to sleep with open doors. (Mr A.S.)

Mr A.C.

Mr A.C. was born in Princess Street in the 1940s. His grandparents, who were good, hard-working people, brought him up. His grandfather was a caretaker and his grandmother a char and although they were poor they had a homely and down-to-earth way of life. Mr A.C. especially enjoyed the community spirit that had been built up over generations. As a young man growing up in Claremont in the 1950s he enjoyed playing soccer and rugby for the Wesley United clubs and meeting his friends on a street corner for a smoke. There was no stigma attached to having a drink in the shebeens either. His great passion in life was 'rock 'n' roll' and he was the lead vocalist for the Swifts. The guys on the corner would rag him and say, 'Hey Elvis, sing us a song'. The Swifts would perform on stage two or three times a year at the Janet Bourhill community centre. After winning the Gold Dollar talent contest in front of a packed audience at the Orpheum cinema, band

members had to run for their lives when members of a losing band chased them.

Claremont provided Mr A.C. with a support network and his teenage years were happy ones. His wife-to-be grew up two streets away. He never foresaw that one day his life would be broken into pieces. After the Group Areas Act was introduced and people started to move out, Claremont lost its atmosphere and became a ghost town. 'People tend to say who favour the National Party viewpoint and there's many, they tend to say that the National Party prevented slums, but the system was very wrong. The whole system was wrong. Coloured men were regarded as second-class citizens. When the City Council built the townships, they built three things. They built the bottle store, the church and the jail. When a man gets thrown out of Claremont, he doesn't know anyone, starts off with new people, new ideas, he gets frustrated, goes and drinks and gets into trouble. Next thing he is in jail, the system is very clever, the system is evil.'

Getting ready to move from Pembroke Street

(Photograph: Don Pinnock)

Several interviewees echoed the same sentiments:

> The gangs were always respectful. They knew you and they were not violent or vicious. You could always walk in the streets at any time of the night without fear. They were not out for killing. Their main concerns were about *dagga*, drink, girls, money and gambling. A guy became a gangster because he wanted to become a macho man. Usually he was a school dropout with few skills. If you greeted him properly and spoke to him respectfully, he would respond. (Mr C.I.)

> *Skollies* did not go out to rob a person. They would hang out on street corners. If they knew you they would even help you against someone else. Today they shoot you, rob you. A *skollie* in those days was a decent *skollie*, he only interfered with you when he was drunk. (Mr B.C.)

Gangs seemed to operate as a form of informal policing as most people of the community knew each other and any outsider was easily identified.

But the Group Areas Act and forced removals destabilised the area, as crime began to escalate in the 1970s. A young white couple moved into a renovated cottage and were seen as strangers by the community. They became easy targets. Their home was burgled several times in the first few months as the community began to fragment.[12] Gangs were very much part of a process of community formation in Claremont, where struggles over space and territory existed alongside neighbourliness and solidarity.

Mrs V.D. also viewed life in Claremont in a far less nostalgic and romanticised way than many others. There were certain areas where she would not walk, especially the little back alleys strewn with rubbish. Crime was rife and *dagga* was freely available. 'You could smell the dagga all over Claremont. There was a lot of domestic violence, men abused their wives and children. People today fantasize about their youth. But it wasn't only pretty stories.' The main social issues in lower Claremont were bread and butter ones, literally about putting food on the table. According to Mr A.P. the common denominators in Claremont were poverty and alcohol. When the Group Areas Act began to affect the people it just added to people's problems.

Group Areas and Forced Removals from the 1970s

Claremont was identified as a 'black spot' as early as 1953, when the apartheid government began to express concerns about the squatting of African families in Cape Town suburbs. The entire Claremont area was regarded as valuable real estate and according to one official, the area was ''n baie waardevolle blanke omgewing – hierdie kolle moet verwyder word' [a very valuable white area – these mixed areas must be removed].[13] Many African families lived in and around the area known as Princess Square and they became the first group in lower Claremont to be harassed by apartheid laws. Mr D.M., a young black man, attended high school in Langa and lived in one room with his brother in Rutland Street, sharing the rent and the kitchen with other families. He counted himself lucky to have any accommodation at all as it was very difficult for African people in the 1950s to find housing in Cape Town. An added bonus was that two brothers lived close by in Cambridge Street. Mr D.M. was continually harassed, he would be woken up in the middle of the night by police conducting pass raids until he was finally evicted in 1959 to live in a 'pondok' in the bushes of Nyanga where conditions were so extreme that Claremont seemed like a 'fairy tale village' by comparison. 'At times when I sit down and think at home, then I feel like crying, really feel like crying. The Group Areas was a heartbreak blow to the black community.' It seems that the Claremont community was unable to do anything to prevent this. Mr A.P. felt that people were not actively mobilising in the 1950s and that existing organisations such as the Coloured People's Congress were too insular.

Lower Claremont was declared a white area in November 1969. The Cape Times reported that 'an air of quiet despair hung over the community'.[14] A critical shortage of between 15 000 and 20 000 houses for coloured people already existed in the Cape Peninsula. This probably accounted for the delay in declaring lower Claremont a white area.[15] Many people who had watched the District Six removals unfold could not quite believe that it would ever happen to them. During the 1970s and 1980s a sizeable portion of the coloured community of Claremont was fragmented and moved to new homes all over the Cape Flats – in Manenberg, Hanover Park, Mitchells Plain, Lavender Hill, Grassy Park, Park Town, even as far as Atlantis on the West Coast. Most members of the community were affected, whether they were homeowners, or renting from white, Indian or Muslim landlords or the City Council. Indian and Muslim owners were forced to sell to whites because they could not own property in a white area. White owners renovated the properties, sold for a good profit as property prices rocketed, or charged high rents. The City Council sold to property developers and many houses were demolished and blocks of flats built in their place.[16] Despite all the odds, a handful of families living in Council cottages around Second Avenue survived many attempts to remove them and they remain in their homes to the present day.[17]

The whole process of selling up and moving left many residents feeling bitter and angry. Mr A.C. summed it up perfectly: 'Apartheid was not based on colour, it was based on greed.' According to Mr R.D., an official from the Group Areas Board came and valued people's houses. In 1972 a three-bedroom house was valued at R3 000. Once sold, a time limit was set on moving out. The seller was penalised 25 per cent on any profit made above the valuation price for every year that he or she stayed on. So if homeowners did not move they would be ruined financially.[18]

Many sellers were intimidated into selling by aggressive estate agents who manipulated people's fears and anxieties. The elderly were particularly vulnerable. Homeowners were made cash offers a little above the board valuation. They thought they were getting fortunes but found out too late that they had been exploited. Mrs A.A. recalled angrily that her father was offered 'peanuts' for his house by

Estate agent's sign in Norfolk Street

(Photograph: Don Pinnock)

'white sharks' and had little option but to accept. Mrs M.N.'s elderly father had to sell the home where he had lived his entire life. As a pensioner he was too old to buy and start again. The money he received from the sale of his house was a pittance and he had to move in with her. 'My father was degraded and dehumanised. He was an owner and now he has nothing.' The 'Group' created a climate of mistrust, exploitation and harassment, as white speculators made money in the process of ejecting residents. Mrs L.v.W. expressed her outrage:

> A Scotsman bought those houses and he could come and put us out of our house, we that were born there. Dug trenches in our yard, that man used to terrorise me. We were amongst the last people left. That guy was breaking up the place right on top of us. The first night after we moved out, I just cried and cried.

Homeowners were the first to move out and whites slowly started to take their place. The words of Mr W.R.'s grandmother were prophetic: 'White people coming in is going to make a big change to this area. One of these days they are going to chase us all out.' The next people to be moved were the backyard tenants who were served eviction notices by officials of the Department of Community Development, while the registered tenants were allowed to stay. Officials used scare tactics to get people to move. An inspector would check up every week. 'This furniture was not here last week. There must be other people living here. How can we work the act if you are getting more people to come and stay in your house?' (Mr A.P.). One young woman became a local hero when she took physical action and punched one of the inspectors in the face. The police were called in but neighbours hid her away successfully (Mrs J.G). Mrs R.H.'s brother was

Renovations in Norfolk Street

(Photograph: Don Pinnock)

evicted by his landlord and left sitting on the pavement with all his belongings. Others were bribed to move with promises of better housing. 'Lots of people thought, here is a good opportunity for me to have my own house, to be on my own' (Mr T.v.W.). But this often did not materialise.

Forced Removals: Resistance and Social Costs

Effective resistance to forced removals within the Claremont community did not occur. Many people felt helpless and scared. This was a time of intense government repression with bannings, detention without trial and police raids, and there were many risks attached to being an activist (Mr A.H.). Political activists such as Dr Alexander and Mr Fataar, both teachers at Livingstone High School at the time, paid a high price for opposing the government. Dr Alexander was banned and

imprisoned on Robben Island. Mr Fataar was forced into exile. He was served his banning orders at Livingstone High School and remembers, 'A policeman named Spyker van Wyk walked into my room. I said, "Oh! Are you coming about Sunday's meeting?" He said. "No, something else with Mr Vorster's signature on it."' 'The average person was too scared to speak out, too afraid of losing his job and family. Besides, the daily struggle of providing food and shelter left most people with little time to worry about anything else' (Mr A.H.). Protest meetings and marches to Parliament were organised by teachers and professional people, but support from the community was not consolidated. This movement was further weakened when many prominent people emigrated.[19] Mr A.P. felt that political parties such as the Unity Movement were out of touch with the needs of the community and were too sophisticated in their approach: 'They spoke about organising boycotts against the removals, but they did not appeal to the ordinary man in the street. The Unity Movement was all unity and no movement. It was an extremely sophisticated group who criticised from a dizzy height.'

In some cases people were just not kept informed about the state of affairs. Mr W.R. felt that the City Council could have done far more in stopping the government from pushing people out of the area. The perception was that the councillors paid lip service to the residents.

> You give them your details and your grievances, why we don't want to move, we just wanted them to listen, to show interest. We had a meeting. That was the start of their back door business. They were not there for the community. When we went there with our grievances, everything was cut and dried, finished, sewn up. We just had to get out. They made every effort to get us out there and get us into Newfields or Hanover Park, whatever. The first thing they will say, *ja* [yes] they got pressurised from the government otherwise they won't get subsidised. They listened to your grievances but did absolutely nothing. (Mr W.R.)

Mr W.R. also recalled that the priest at St Ignatius Catholic Church tried to buy some of the properties, but was told quite clearly by the City Council that if the houses were not to be occupied by whites, there was no sense in buying them.

The financial costs of the forced removals were a real burden as so many people were poor. People were plagued by unnecessary new expenses and often plunged into debt. Many could barely afford the costs of moving their household goods. Monthly rents increased dramatically. People had to fork out money for electricity deposits and new telephones. Council houses had no chimneys. Previously people cooked on wood or coal stoves. Now they needed to buy expensive gas or electrical appliances. Mrs G.A. had to move her children out of Livingstone High School because she could not afford the new transport costs from her new home on the Cape Flats to Claremont.

> The high school was right in our road. It took three minutes to get there. The children still stayed on at Livingstone when we moved out. But we are a big family and the train fares were just too expensive. I was very heartsore when my children were forced to come to the local school just to save money. (Mrs G.A.)

But the emotional and psychological costs of resettlement were as severe. According to Mr R.D., 'I don't think the English language was ever invented to describe the variety of pain that people suffered. What was lost was the integrity of the community life, the sense of belonging, of continuity and connectedness. What was lost in lower Claremont was in every way as disastrous as District Six or South End.'[20]

Mr A.C. describes the 'Group' as a system as evil as Nazism. For him Manenberg was an inconvenient and dangerous place where he felt isolated and frustrated.

> It takes a lot of nerve and a lot of courage to be uprooted and then told you must start again. The National Party took away our roots, our atmosphere. Harfield Village today is almost unrecognisable. I have often asked

myself, do whites console themselves, we bought this property, we never stole it from them? I get very emotional. This place was like a human feeling, when I moved out I was completely shattered.

For Mrs R.H., going back to see the old house where she was born was a painful experience. The pomegranate tree is still growing in the backyard. 'I don't want to go back to Harfield. You can't get better memories than that. It is not the same, it is too quiet, there is nothing going on, now it is dead, dead, dead.'

As a result of the Group Areas Act, there were at least 11 800 coloured families evicted from the Cape Town area.[21] This included many lower Claremont residents, although the exact numbers are unknown. What comes through clearly in the interviews is the overwhelming sense of loss, both for the physical place and for the bonds of community, friendship and fellowship that were so carelessly broken by the apartheid regime. Mr A.S.'s words serve as a indictment of the racial policies of the Nationalist government:

> Because you must be honest, there are decent people everywhere, all kinds to make a world, whether you are pink, blue, yellow or black, it makes no difference. We all have to form society and those years, look we were living in the apartheid era, so we kept to ourselves. I still tell them up to today – you know these whites, you know what separated us from whites in Claremont? A wall. What? A wall. Gloucester Street had a wall. Then the whites used to come by the wall and call over, 'Aunty, Aunty come do my washing'. That was a wall because of them being white and we being coloured, but we were friends, we were friends ... until today we are still friends and some of them are directors and stuff, you know big boys, lawyers and stuff. We still know each other, nothing wrong, that was the only thing to say, with just that wall and it was wicked. Oh! Hold it. I don't want to be a politician, but it was wicked to see us having to live one side of the wall you know

Mrs A.A.

Mrs A.A. was born in Lansdowne in 1945. Her father owned their house in York Street and she grew up there. Her father was a carpenter and her grandfather was a priest at the Harvey Road mosque. When her father could not obtain any building work her mother found temporary work in a clothing factory. One of Mrs A.A.'s chores as a child was to see that a bath of hot water would always be ready for her father when he came home from work. Their house did not have a bathroom or running water. She would fill the galvanised iron bath with hot water from the boiler next to the coal stove in the kitchen. A typical family meal was soup, sweet potatoes and *vetkoek*. The family would say prayers and sing Muslim hymns together. She attended All Saints School and enjoyed the Christmas carols and Easter celebrations, but was always a Muslim first. Eid was an important celebration for her family. As a child she would visit neighbours and say *slamat*. Any pennies she received would be handed over to her mother. She remembers queuing at Harfield Road Station early in the morning for rations of butter, rice and *mielie* (maize) meal and fetching fresh milk from the dairy in Second Avenue. She enjoyed eating the delicious *tameletjies* made by a neighbour. These consisted of roasted pine kernels set in a sugar syrup. They were sold wrapped up in small squares of exercise book paper.

She left Oaklands High School in Standard Seven (Grade Nine) at the age of 15 and went to work as a factory worker for Barkers shoe factory. Her pay was given to her mother, who in return would give her pocket money. Because of her religious beliefs she did not attend any dances or parties, but enjoyed going to the cinema on a Saturday afternoon. Claremont was a place where she felt safe as a young woman. There was always a good atmosphere, everything was close by and convenient and she was able to walk around freely.

and they would come to our side towards First Avenue come to Bell Road and they would come in First Avenue, down First Avenue to watch the coons. They are white, we are black or coloured. There wasn't the in-fighting that people would have expected, you know, but it's only as it's all built up over the years. I was born in the apartheid era ... it takes all kinds to make a world.

But there is another positive theme that is woven into these life histories. Claremont people have proved to be remarkably resilient. They have overcome adversity and rebuilt their lives. Many people still maintain links with Claremont by remaining in contact with old friends, or meet again at functions such as weddings and funerals. In spite of the distance from their homes in suburbs such as Hanover Park, Mitchells Plain and Grassy Park, some former residents still attend religious services at the churches and mosque (Mr A.P.). Schools such as Rosmead Primary and Livingstone High have survived the apartheid years and continue to flourish and provide educa-

tion for the grandsons and granddaughters of old Claremont residents. So, there is some sense of continuity. People, despite the unbelievable odds, manage to hold on to their history.

In September 1999, the first land and property claims in lower Claremont were settled. Without doubt this financial restitution will help to bring some sense of social justice to the people who suffered under apartheid. But for many other Claremont residents, telling personal stories and remembering their former lives offer a means of coming to terms with the loss of their homes. That this past was filled with injustice is very evident in the often angry and emotional stories recounted here. In sharp contrast, memories of life in lower Claremont before removals are filled with nostalgia and portray a world of community cohesion and solidarity. In powerful ways, memories are life-sustaining forces that provide meaning in a world that is sometimes hard to understand. This essay has only touched on the wealth of human experience that made up this working-class community of Cape Town. It is hoped that in some small way, it will add to an understanding of this cultural heritage.

8 | 'I dream of our old house, you see there are things that can never go away': Memory, Restitution and Democracy[1]

Sean Field

The residents of Windermere, Tramway Road, District Six, Simon's Town and lower Claremont experienced the pain and sadness of forced removals. The communities in which people lived before forced removals were either lost or destroyed by the actions of the apartheid state. But a sense of community belonging and identity has been kept alive through people's memories of the time before forced removals and by hopes and dreams for a better future. For some people, dreams of returning to their old homes will 'never go away'. As this book draws to a close, we explore how these popular memories and events of the past are influencing the present.

Memories Are Who We Are

Memories, ja, wat nooit, wat kan weggaan nie. Die enigste tyd wat dit by jou sal weggaan, as jy onner die sand komberse gaan, dan sal dit natuurlik nou weggaan. Maar soe lank jy leef is daar dinge, wat vir jou verinner, van daardie dae. Jy kom by plekke wat jy onthou, hier was ek nog kind, hier't ek nog dit gedoen, daar het dat gedoen, hier't ek gehardloop en soe aan. Nog baie dinge wat jou vir aandagtelik maak, wat jy nie kan vergeet nie. [Memories, yes, that never, that can't go away. The only time it will leave you is when you are under the sand blankets, then it will naturally go away. But as long as*

you live there are things which remind you of those days. You come to places that you remember, here I was still a child, here I did this, there I did that, here I used to run and so on. Still lots of things that make you thoughtful, which you will never forget. (Mr D.S., former Windermere resident)

Mr D.S. presents a persuasive case for the power of memory and space. But the places in our minds and bodies where we retain memories do not work like an auto-teller machine at the bank. Memories are sets of thoughts, images and feelings about the past. We forget our memories because of old age or illness. We avoid reliving our memories because they are too painful, sad or shameful. And now and then we silence our memories because it is too threatening to think or speak about them. People remember in different ways. But we still need shared memories of people, places and events to understand who and what we have become.

People sustain and express their memories through talking, writing, drawing, photography, video, performances and many other art forms. Storytelling is a fundamental way of constructing memories for other audiences. The interviewees in this book have drawn on their memories to tell their life stories. While doing so they have either changed or forgotten some of their memories. The patterns of memory are partly influenced by external audiences and the speaker's mood at the time of telling the story. The patterns of memory are also partly influenced by the individual's need to be heard, seen and remembered.

People often describe their memories in nostalgic and romantic ways such as 'everything was nice then' or 'we always lived happily together then'. Many academics have rejected these kinds of memory as unreliable or false.[2] In this book we have argued that it is of limited value to understand memories only through scientific definitions of what is true or false. It is far more useful to record and interpret how people make their own truths and their own meanings. These personalised constructions of memories are created in particular social contexts.

Social contexts consist of the multiple relationships in which we live, play, study and work, and the literature we read, the television and movies we watch, and the performances we observe. The words, languages and stories we learn are also drawn from these differing contexts. These contextual relationships shape us as social people and influence how we remember, forget, silence and understand the past. For example, under apartheid people often remembered, or only spoke about, the memories or beliefs that they thought were safe to express in the context of political repression.

A central purpose of this book is to encourage young and old to communicate their memories from person to person, generation to generation, and community to community. Without the help of other people, how can we be sure of the public value of our memories? We need to express our memories so that others can reflect back at us who we are and how we are. In short, people tend to remember what they need to remember for interwoven personal and social purposes. For these needs to be fulfilled, we require others to listen to our memories and stories, whether the events that are remembered occurred earlier today or decades ago.

'Remembering Is So Good Because We Are Helping One Another'

When people were forcibly removed they lost their land, property and many other possessions.

But people also lost a home, a community and even a sense of family and friendship. When ties to home and community are broken, strong feelings are stirred up, which can range from hurt, sadness and vulnerability to guilt and anger. In the process of recording memory it is important that we do not avoid these feelings and emotions.

The ways in which people define a sense of home and community are deeply connected to their sense of self and the areas in which they played and worked, and where they turned certain spaces into their 'turf', 'stomping ground' or 'neighbourhood'. What we remember of these places and spaces includes images, smells, tastes and sounds we experienced there. There are many things in our current lives that can act as triggers for these memories to reappear, for example, meeting someone from the old area or seeing an old photograph. Or it might happen through hearing a story or seeing a familiar object like a domestic implement. Group interactions also encourage the reappearance of memories.

You know people they always remind one another where they used to stay, because there is a burial society for Windermere people. If they were staying in Windermere they all come together, in the meetings here in this hall here. We know one another. We have got the burial society of Windermere. Like others in Retreat also have people, who used to stay in Retreat, they are reminding each other and they also build up a burial society. Whoever passed away they come here. We are doing collections and burying each other, one another ... remembering is so good because we are helping one another. That's what, we are not forgetting one another, when we come together even here in Guguletu. (Mr A.Z., former Windermere resident)

The social relationships construct the spaces and places where memories are regularly triggered or communicated. And these symbolic spaces where memories cluster can become a site of popular memory. A site of memory can be a physical place where an historical event occurred. Or it can be the history of a family, a community, an organisation or a group of people who have shared memories. The communities from which people were forcibly removed, and the places they were moved to, are important sites of popular memory from the apartheid era. The most well-known example of a site of popular memory in Cape Town is the space where District Six once stood. This space is now mostly rubble and weeds, but this large scar is a reminder to most Capetonians of the forced removal of District Six residents. Sites of memory have the potential to conserve the physical, social and emotional aspects of memory. They also have the potential to incorporate individual life stories into collective forms of memory.

For memory to be popular, public or collective, and for these memories to be sustained, requires relationships between people – relationships in which people feel comfortable telling their stories and others feel comfortable listening to them. When former residents talk about the past it is common for people to refer to themselves as 'District Sixers', or 'Windermere people', to name but two examples. Popular memory mostly relies on people's struggles to express their feelings of togetherness and belonging. Through people expressing memories about their shared past, collective forms of identity, like a community identity, are kept alive. The communities we have explored in this book might be physically 'lost', but former residents continue to sustain and express their memories as a community-in-memory.

A community-in-memory is usually shaped around the experience of loss. But a community-in-memory is also a brave and creative response to this loss, which allows people to move into the future without forgetting or denying their shared past. It is impossible to use numbers, rands or cents to exactly measure the emotional loss that survivors of forced removals suffered. However, forms of restitution are not only appropriate but fully justified for the survivors of forced removals.

Restitution: Laws and Experiences

Between 1913 and 1983 at least 3,9 million people were forcibly removed in South Africa. With the transition to democratic government, a land reform programme was developed by the Department of Land Affairs to deal with these exploitative land practices.[3] In 1994 the Restitution of Land Rights Act was passed by Parliament. The Act is relevant to people dispossessed of property through racist laws or practices after 19 June 1913 and entitles people to either receive their original land or alternative state land. For many others, restitution will involve the payment of financial compensation.

The Act created two structures: the Commission on Restitution of Land Rights (CRLR) and the Land Claims Court. The Land Claims Court makes judgements about land claims and what kind of restitution will be granted. The Commission helps claimants and prepares cases for judgement by the Land Claims Court.[4] Claimants can be individuals, co-owners, a group or a whole community. The Act was designed to reduce conflict and produce fair agreement between all parties. The claim for restitution is therefore not against individuals or communities but against the state, which pays for restitution. The restitution process is rooted in the principle 'right in land'. This right refers to property owners and tenants.[5] Tenants only qualify if their tenancy was for a continuous period of not less than ten years prior to dispossession.[6] It is important to note that the Act does not give preference to property owners.[7]

Most cases require time-consuming archival research to verify claims. Under apartheid, property owners and labour tenants were officially recorded, whereas many residential tenants were not.[8] In these kinds of cases oral testimony can help establish whether a claim is valid and what form of restitution is to be provided. Oral history testimony is legally recognised in the Land Claims Court.

Democratically organised community initiatives which resolve divisive interests will have a greater chance of successful restitution. While claimants in rural and some urban areas might get their original land back, in most urban areas claimants are more likely to get financial compensation. In the Cape Town urban context there are many areas where it will be impossible for people to return to their original houses or land. For example, where Ndabeni residents used to live there are now several factories; many upper Claremont residents used to live where Cavendish Square shopping mall is today; the new Cape Technikon takes up a large portion of what was once District Six. In some areas, for example, parts of Tramway Road and District Six, claimants will eventually receive new houses on the original land. In respect of communities discussed in Chapters 3 to 7, the following number of claims have been lodged (the names of support groups constituted by claimants are given in brackets):[9]

- Windermere–Kensington: 600 (The Kensington–Factreton Restitution Committee)
- Tramway Road: 115 (The Return to Tramways Committee)[10]
- District Six: 2 500 (The District Six Beneficiaries Trust)
- Simon's Town: 700 (The South Peninsula Land Claims Committee)[11]
- Claremont: 358 (The Harfield Village Restitution Committee).[12]

On a national level, 970 claims out of 63 455 claims have been completed. In the Western Cape region 46 out of 11 938 (595 rural and 11 343 urban) claims have been resolved.[13] The lengthy restitution process has been frustrating for many claimants. A Tramway Road resident said: 'Nothing has happened for a year and people have already passed away. We have done all our homework, we want to be role-players but we can't move forward.'[14] Uncertainty about how to compensate tenants is one of the problems which have delayed the process. Other problems have ranged from a too legalistic approach and the massive load of research required. To speed up the restitution process, the Commission was integrated into the Department of Land Affairs in 1999. The restitution process has also been refined to facilitate the efficient administrative resolution of claims.

We need to acknowledge that the survivors of forced removals have been suffering for many years and it is not surprising that they want restitution to happen without delay. As many survivors have said to me, 'If they say I can go back, I want to be number one back.'[15] Sadly, there will be no instant relief from the emotional burden of the past. Many people have refused to apply for restitution because it is too difficult for them to relive uncomfortable memories. And many others who did apply have said that it has made their emotional burden even worse. The legal demand for restitution and the emotional need for healing overlap in tension-ridden ways within the restitution process. Nevertheless, people's struggles for restitution are driven by dreams of returning to the home or community where they feel they belonged. But this struggle is also about wanting to be heard, wanting to be seen, and wanting to be remembered.

Living Heritage, Healing and Development

Heritage is not only about monuments, museums, statues and objects. The memories and stories presented in this book are significant parts of a living heritage inside people. Living heritage is also about the social connections and cultural relationships between people. People express themselves through gossip, folklore, urban legends, traditions and other forms of storytelling. These are the colourful threads that weave the fabric of communities. But stories can only survive if there are relationships through which they can be communicated. Forced removals shattered many of these relationships and as a result many memories have disappeared over time. Nevertheless, communities who were previously destroyed can revive a community identity through talking about their shared past.

Oral and audio-visual history methods can contribute to this through the recording of exciting sounds and images of the past. Concrete examples include community radio, video and storyboards. Oral history can also be used in identifying key buildings to be declared community monuments, and setting up local museums or exhibitions in schools, libraries and old-age homes. Residents and students, with the assistance of local teachers, librarians or social workers, could create audio-visual exhibitions around various themes of a community's history.

Oral histories presented through community exhibitions and commemorative ceremonies have the potential to trigger people's memories and revive a sense of togetherness. In the process, people draw on local forms of knowledge about their current community and the communities from which they were forcibly removed. For example, the District Six Museum continuously attracts former residents to see its exhibitions and to talk about their memories. As a former resident said, 'The day I left our house in District Six, never to return, I knew my life had changed forever ... I thought my happiness had received a blow from which it would never recover. Who would have thought that, with the establishment of the District Six Museum, there would be a return of meaning into my life?'[16] The District Six Museum also runs a District Six and Beyond Campaign and has hosted an exhibition on the Tramway Road community. Through exhibitions, music and heritage workshops, the District Six Museum has become a rallying point for the commemoration of popular memories of the Cape Flats and other parts of Cape Town.

Many other communities also need to be assisted in recording and passing on their stories about community life and forced removals. The present Bonteheuwel community consists of people forcibly removed from District Six, Tramway Road, Mowbray and many other places. In Section 2, Guguletu, most of the elderly residents were either removed from Windermere–Kensington or Blouvlei–Retreat. The original Langa residents were from Ndabeni and Windermere and other parts of Cape Town. The Gugusi'thebe Project has built a tourist centre which will ultimately include a museum, restaurant and heritage walks around historical sites in Langa.

On an individual level, we need to remember that numerous former residents of District Six, Windermere, Kensington, Harfield and Simon's Town are elderly and are often physically or emotionally frail. Through oral storytelling about the past, the elderly can regain and defend their sense

of self. Talking to friends and relatives, giving oral history interviews and speaking to social workers are some of the ways in which reminiscence can help. '[We need] to be reminded of the distance which sometimes stretches between generations. It's a distance which can feel painful if it means a feeling of exclusion and the loss of a sense of value.'[17] The community, especially the youth, needs to be encouraged to either tape-record or write down the stories of elderly residents and to collect their old family photographs, letters and objects.

This book has demonstrated that the losses people suffered were not only material in nature, but also involved distressing feelings. The land or money people receive through the restitution process will help. But land or financial compensation will only partly resolve people's emotional burdens. Talking to people (professionals, family or friends) will provide some release and temporary comfort to former residents. Through this sharing, survivors of forced removals will see and hear that they are not alone in experiencing these feelings. Regaining a sense of collectivity and community spirit will help people to cope with their devastating emotional losses.

An extremely painful theme, which this book has not dealt with, are the various forms of violence that were central to forced removals across South Africa. The stories of Crossroads residents in Cape Town are filled with images of violence:

> I encountered severe problems during all the incidents of violence that took place here, especially the 1993 violence, which left scars in my heart. Last year we were attacked by Nongwe's group, claiming that the land we were occupying was going to be developed and houses built, so we must move ... we said, before we can do so, he must bring back those who were removed in 1992, and he ignored that and called his men to burn the houses. And we were shot by policemen to move away from Section 2. As a result, my first-born daughter was shot by the police. She even saw the number plate of that casspir. That same year my last-born was slaughtered by Nongwe's men. (Ms Q.)[18]

Residents often talk about feeling 'bad' about what happened to them under apartheid. The word 'bad' seems to cover a large number of feelings which many people find difficult to name and express. Feelings like hurt, sadness, shame, guilt, emptiness and much more are just some of the unsettling feelings that the apartheid state inflicted on people. A well-trained oral history interviewer (and other empathic listeners) can help people to talk about and name some of these feelings in the safety of the interview situation. Allowing individuals the space to express their memories, filled with feelings, can make small contributions to healing, but deeper healing may take many years.[19]

A former resident of the Bo-Kaap, who could not read or write, described the recording of oral history interviews in the community as follows: 'Soe jy gaan bietjie vat van daai een en daai een, dan sit jy dit in 'n groot pot, en kook dit, en dan voer jy almal.' [So you take a little bit from that one and from that one, then you put it in a big pot, and cook it, and then you feed everyone.] While oral historians cannot meet these high expectations, these words do illustrate a significant point about oral history. Oral history, when publicly presented, can help people to connect with each other. Piecing together parts of a community history has the potential to help bridge divisions inside and between communities. It might enable communities to rebuild damaged or broken relationships between families, friends, neighbours and generations.

Urban renewal and community development requires concrete and bricks but also involves the rebuilding of community, cultural and social relationships. As one developer has argued, 'If oral history techniques are institutionalised in project work, they can increase understanding and sensitivity towards the participating community.'[20] What communities think, feel and remember can hold crucial lessons for how communities need to be serviced and developed by government departments and community developers.

Democracy: Struggles against Forgetting and Silencing

Is oral history democratic? Oral history can be used to achieve either democratic or undemocratic political goals. As oral history is not automatically democratic we need to work at using it for democratic purposes. Some of the small ways in which oral history contributes to democracy include helping people to find their voices and express themselves with confidence, and ensuring that others listen to these stories.

When recording a community history it is crucial to explore ways of including the many, and at times competing, voices and interests which make up all communities. The community never speaks with a single voice. By silencing conflicting opinions and memories, we do the community a disservice and we are not promoting democratic values. For example, it is often believed that only people classified coloured and white lived in District Six, when, in fact, this is not true. This was Nomvuyo Ngcelwane's reaction to the news that Africans removed from District Six qualified for restitution:

> [It was] really surprising, since it is seldom
> if ever acknowledged that Africans, too, used
> to live in District Six. People only know of
> the experiences of their former coloured
> neighbours ... it is often forgotten that we
> hold the same sentiments about the place as
> them. Don't we? How on earth can I be
> expected to forget twenty years of my life?
> That's ridiculous.[21]

Today it is possible to enter an evocative exhibition called 'Nomvuyo's room' at the District Six Museum. We need to use oral history and complementary methods like visual history to record and interpret the hidden stories and memories inside communities. What of the silenced histories of women and gay, lesbian and disabled people who live in all these communities? Oral history, combined with effective community heritage strategies, can help promote greater tolerance between people of different orientations and political, cultural, religious or social beliefs. But the potential of oral history is hampered by various obstacles preventing people from remembering the past.

A tendency to forget the past is a natural part of growing old. As people die, memories disappear. Also, the fear of speaking about memories that might reflect negatively on others will continue to silence people. In some cases, censorship and silencing is still being imposed by powerful leaders or warlords. Members of both the apartheid and even the post-apartheid government are often more comfortable with a cleaned-up, official version of the past. The critical reactions of both the National Party and the African National Congress to the final report of the Truth and Reconciliation Commission (TRC) illustrate this point.

Oral history, in part, can be used to oppose these trends. The past is not an object just waiting to be discovered, dusted off and documented. How we remember, record and interpret the past makes history open to contestation. Instead of creating the impression that there is only one version of the past, such as apartheid historians did, we need to encourage the democratic inclusion of multiple views of the past. This is not simply an academic question of interpretation. The approach to or versions of the apartheid past that wins this contest will have an impact on:

- the allocation of land and compensation
- the development of heritage sites and resources
- the distribution of reparations and welfare resources
- the socio-economic development of communities, and
- how we define ourselves as individuals, communities and as a country.

This book ends with feelings of both optimism and pessimism. Optimism because real changes are occurring in people's lives, with the help of the restitution process, the TRC and development projects. Pessimism because these activities will not take away the trauma and other feelings with which people still live. These feelings of the survivors are aggravated by the fact that the people who committed human rights abuses through forced removals will probably escape justice. Should there be a TRC-type process for the survivors and perpetrators of forced removals? At the very least, much more oral history and memory work needs to be done with the survivors of forced removals throughout South Africa.

These mixed feelings are also rooted in the ongoing struggles against forgetting and silencing. We must not forget the thousands of other stories of people who were scattered all over the Cape Flats and beyond. Who will listen to the stories of the people who were forcibly 'endorsed out' to the rural areas of the Eastern and Northern Cape? And, who will listen to the people who were removed to Bonteheuwel, Manenberg, Bishop Lavis, Hanover Park, Bridgetown, Langa, Guguletu, Khayelitsha and many other communities? In addition, a future project of the Centre for Popular Memory is to record and disseminate the memories of people who experienced forced removals in the northern suburbs of Cape Town.

Finally, our democracy should not be taken for granted or assumed to be enough. By telling stories across communities and generations we can strengthen popular memory and deepen the democracy that so many people before us struggled for.

Appendix
Oral History Projects
Sean Field

We practise oral history when we talk about the past to friends, family members, colleagues or anyone else. While we might not call it 'oral history', we all use oral history as a part of our daily lives. Oral history as a lived practice existed long before academics thought of and developed 'oral history' as a research practice. Oral history as a research method only began in the 1950s in the United States of America and the United Kingdom, and became a popular method for progressive academics and students in the 1960s. A central reason for this growth was the production of cheap hand-held tape recorders. During the 1970s, as the South African trade union movement began to rebuild itself, oral history became especially popular amongst trade unionists and adult educators. Since then, oral history as a research practice has been used in universities, schools, museums and many non-governmental organisations across South Africa.

Oral history as a research method records the spoken memories and stories of people in the interview situation. The interview usually takes place in a room, but could also happen in the open air. The interview can be recorded by means of handwritten notes, but it is far more efficient to use either a tape recorder or video camera. Once interviews are recorded, the tapes are transcribed and interpreted, and then they are usually used to write up a research project. But oral history also refers to the ways in which memories and stories are passed on to the public through archives, books, films, television, radio and community drama.[1] You do not need to be a professional to do an oral history project. This appendix describes some guidelines for oral history interviewing and provides tips for an oral history project on forced removals.[2]

Planning Your Oral History Project

It is very common for researchers to have ambitious research aims that they fail to achieve because they did not plan their project carefully enough. A research plan should include a clear research focus, budget and timetable. It is important to have a flexible plan that allows for unpredictable events. But oral history research should be conducted in an organised and disciplined manner if it is to be given the recognition it deserves. The following questions need to be confronted:

- **What are the central goals of your research project?**
  Tips: Think carefully about and write down your central goals. Make sure these goals are realistic. Rather have a few, narrowly defined goals. Define your goals in terms of the central research questions to be answered. Consider what format you want to produce the project in, for example a booklet or video. Bear in mind who you are and how your age, race, gender or educational level might affect your research. Think about which audiences will read, see or hear your project.
- **What is the best research method to meet your goals?**
  Tips: Oral history is good for recording memories and exploring topics about people's experiences. But it is often necessary to use other research methods too. For example, collecting newspaper clippings, photographs and written documents can improve the quality of your interviews.
- **How much time and what resources are required to complete the project?**
  Tips: Compile a budget for all your possible expenses, listing how you are going to pay for

them as well as any income you might earn from the project. Write up a timetable with due dates for specific tasks and for the completion of the final project. Research is time-consuming, so always allow for enough time.

- **How will you distribute the findings of your project?**

  Tips: Consult the interviewees and ask them how they would like to see their stories taken forward. It is crucial to include this aspect of oral history work in your plan, budget and timetable.

Equipment

A tape recorder to record interviews is preferable. A hand-held recorder or a portable radio-tape deck are both suitable. However, the quality of the recording is often poor on this kind of equipment. The best way to overcome this limitation is to buy a hand-held microphone or, preferably, a lapel microphone. These are expensive items and you might need to loan them from a company, school or university that hires out equipment. A portable video camera can also be used. The video camera is very effective in capturing the facial expressions and bodily mannerisms of the interviewee, but can make some interviewees uncomfortable.

For the transcription of your interviews you could use your tape recorder or video camera but this is very time-consuming and costly. It is far more efficient to buy or loan a transcribing machine.[3] Make sure the transcriber has headphones (for better listening), a foot pedal (to control the movement of the tape) and a speed control function. Always use normal-size tape cassettes (not the mini-cassettes) as they are more common and tend to be more durable. Use 60-minute tapes instead of 90-minute tapes, as these are less likely to stretch. Chrome tapes are more expensive than carbon tapes, but survive longer, and are therefore better for archival purposes. Always make back-up copies of your interviews and rather work with your back-up copies and not the originals. If you are fortunate to have a large budget, then the most up-to-date technology to buy would be mini-disks (very similar to CDs) or a digital audio-recorder.

Selecting Interviewees

When drawing up your research project plan (goals, methodology, budget and timetable) you need to decide whom you are going to interview. One way of beginning this is to do a single life history – consisting of several interviews – with an elderly family member or person in your neighbourhood. Or you could conduct a small case study on forced removals by interviewing all the older members of your family or residents of your street. If you want to document the whole or a part of your community's history, then you will need to decide what your main themes are. Here are some questions you will need to confront when selecting interviewees:

- How long did they reside in the communities they were removed from?
- Will you select an equal number of male and female interviewees?
- Will you select interviewees according to race, ethnicity or culture?
- Will you select people according to their class or economic positions?
- Will you select them according to age and generation?
- Are you interested in their political affiliations?
- Are you interested in their religious affiliations?
- How important are sports and cultural club memberships?

These questions will cover the most common possibilities or variables when developing a community research project on forced removals. If you are unable to select interviewees according to all these possibilities, you then will have to prioritise the themes that are essential to your project.

These possibilities (phrased as questions) must correspond to your central research goals. For example, if one of your central goals is to find out whether men and women in your community remember forced removals in different ways, then consider the following analytical question: Do men and women have similar or different ways of remembering their experiences of forced removals? This question could be followed up with such questions as, Why do these differences and similarities in remembering the past happen? These analytical questions will guide you in your approach to the interviews. It is preferable to find people who are comfortable with talking about themselves and others, and they should have relatively clear memories of the past. But as memory is open to change you cannot be rigid about this. You need to adopt flexible strategies in setting up and conducting interviews.

Setting up Interviews

Interviews are set up and conducted on the basis of a clear understanding that the interviewee has information which you, the interviewer, do not have.[4] Therefore it is important to gain permission to interview people in a sensitive way. Bear in mind that the interviewees are doing you a favour by giving up their time to tell their stories for your research project.

By stressing that your project is contributing to a shared heritage of the community, you are more likely to get a co-operative response from potential interviewees. When conducting interviews in communities, it is necessary to first get permission from the organisational gatekeepers of the community. These might be the civic associations, political groups or local municipal councillors. Once organisational clearance is obtained, the researcher needs to get potential interviewees to agree to be interviewed.

Another central issue to consider when setting up an interview is to establish which language will be spoken during the interview. Generally, interviewees prefer to use their first language. It is obviously preferable if the interviewer can speak the interviewee's first language. In situations where this is not possible, there are at least two options: a translator could be used, or the interview could be conducted in a language other than the first language of the interviewee.[5] Both options have their advantages and disadvantages. The translator option often hinders the negotiation of an intimate interviewer–interviewee relationship and immediate translation is often inaccurate. But this option allows the interviewee the comfort of using his or her first language. Conversely, speaking in a language other than his or her first language is often

uncomfortable for the interviewee and there can be misunderstandings of words or cultural dynamics.

There is an additional local issue that crops up when interviewing someone in his or her own African language: while using the mother tongue of the interviewee is good for interviewing, it limits the breadth of audiences that can be reached through dissemination. In short, there is a tension to be resolved: using the interviewee's first language is usually best for interviewing, but using a dominant language like English is usually best for dissemination purposes.

Before you start interviewing, it is also important to form a verbal contract with the interviewee that deals with the issue of confidentiality. This means you need interviewees' permission to use their names in your project. Alternatively, you must keep interviewees' names separate from their stories. Many interviewees feel more comfortable talking on tape if you are not going to use their names. But sometimes, if the interviewee is famous or well known in the community, this might not be possible. The interviewee should also be informed that he or she has the right to choose not to answer any questions or end the interview at any time he or she chooses.

When the interview has been completed, ask the interviewee to complete a written contract. This is either an interviewee–interviewer agreement or a release form. This legal agreement gives the copyright to the researcher, but also gives the interviewee the chance to place any restrictions on the recorded stories. Interviewees may choose to allow the stories to be used only for educational and not for commercial purposes. The interviewees might also choose to withhold the whole interview or parts of the interview from being published for a certain number of years.

While setting up and doing the interview, try to present yourself in a confident but humble and respectful manner. The more you can consult with interviewees about the project, the better. This is especially important if your central aim is to establish a history over which the community has a greater degree of control. However, extensive consultation is often frustrating and time-consuming. At the very least, your guiding aim should be to develop open and honest dialogues with interviewees.

Doing Interviews

Before you start interviewing, write up an 'interview guide'. The interview guide is not a fixed schedule, but should be seen as a checklist or a safety net to help with asking questions. The content and the manner in which interview questions are asked will help the interviewee to relax into a storytelling mood. It is essential to ask questions that do not appear on your interview guide such as questions for clarification and questions that link with what the interviewee has previously spoken about. This shows that you are really interested in what the interviewee has to say and will facilitate further storytelling.

When conducting a research project on a community that experienced forced removals, we recommend the life story interview guide. A life story interview can be roughly chronological, but in fact, it often follows a more inconsistent order. This approach tends to work well because it allows people more space to narrate their memories and to move around from topic to topic and from one time period to another. This flexible approach also allows the interviewee time to feel more comfortable with the interview situation. People's stories also connect to their memories of living as members of communities, families, organisations, teams and cultural groups. The life story interview guide also helps the interviewer to contextualise and explore these specific community or social themes in more detail.

The interviewer can use many interviewing skills to make the interviewee feel more comfortable. I will mention only two significant skills here. Firstly, the interviewer needs to learn how to be an empathic listener. Interviewees should see and feel that you are really listening to their stories. Secondly, you need to learn how to ask questions in a simple and sensitive way. Try to avoid asking leading questions such as: How bad did you feel when you were forcibly removed? A better way of asking the question would be: How

did you feel when you were forcibly removed? Try to avoid asking more than one question at a time. Also avoid analytical, abstract or long-winded questions such as: What was your class, race and gender consciousness at the time of forced removals? Rather ask short, open-ended questions such as: How do you think forced removals affected your community? What do you think of the people who did these removals?

Interviewers should remember that the information they are requesting is often connected to intense feelings. Oral history interviewing is not the quick journalistic or talk-show style of interviewing. Oral history requires a patient and slow style that is sensitive and respectful of the interviewee's background and mood. This style of interviewing will help the interviewee to tell more intimate stories and details. These stories might not be meaningful to you or others, but it is crucial to give interviewees the time to tell stories that are meaningful to them.

All interviewers, be they experienced or inexperienced, make mistakes. Here are some common mistakes made by interviewers:

- arriving late
- interrupting the interviewee
- talking too much
- trying to solve the interviewee's problems
- interrogating the interviewee
- arguing with the interviewee.

A good oral history interview is based less on right and wrong and more on building trust between yourself and the interviewee. If you deal with your mistakes in an open and sensitive way, it might even benefit your relationship with interviewees. You are not doing a scientific experiment. You are interviewing a person with complex memories and feelings. If interviewees trust you and feel comfortable being interviewed by you, they will gradually reveal meaningful stories that are helpful to both them and you.

Transcribing Interviews

This is probably the most time-consuming part of doing oral history research. Even with a modern transcribing machine, it is reasonable to expect one hour of interviewing time to take four to seven hours of typing time to be transcribed. This transcribing time will mostly depend on the quality of your sound recording. It is essential to have clearly transcribed interviews for most research projects. You must decide whether you need a complete transcript of each interview. If your aim is to get a nearly complete community record, then verbatim transcripts (transcribing every word) are essential. If your aims are more limited, selective transcripts of the sections or responses you intend analysing or quoting for your project are sufficient. Make sure that you keep the tape cassettes (and copies) in a safe place. It is a good idea to label your tapes with the following minimum information: the interviewee's name and contact details; the interviewer's name; the date of the interview; and where it took place.[6]

When transcribing, it is crucial to be aware that there is no one-to-one relationship between the spoken word and the written word. People do not speak as they write. A transcriber-typist can creatively use written words to describe the sounds, expressions and words spoken by the interviewee. The transcriber should also explore ways of describing non-verbal sounds and the mood of the interview dialogue. It is usually better if the interviewer is also the transcriber. Professional typists or transcribers might do the job more neatly and quickly but at an added financial cost.

Disseminating Oral Histories

The stories recorded through the oral history method should be distributed to the individuals and communities where they originated, and to as many other audiences as possible. The central strength of the oral history method is that it usually focuses on recording the many views of people who have been marginalised or oppressed in our society. But researchers have often put insufficient energy and money into disseminating oral histories to communities and the broader public.

Oral histories of communities who experienced forced removals have been recorded through different media, for example, popular history books such as this book and video documentaries like *The Last Supper at Horstley Street*. Other examples are community radio programmes broadcast by Bush Radio in Cape Town. If you write up a school or university research project it is a good idea to offer interviewees a copy of their interview tapes. While the written medium is useful, I strongly recommend that you rather use audio-recordings or audio-visual mediums so that oral histories can be heard or seen by as many other people as possible. For example, you could use your interviews to make a radio or video programme of fifteen to thirty minutes. Try to make sure that the tapes and transcripts are lodged with an archive. By placing your interviews in a sound or audio-visual archive researchers and other members of the public can listen to them and use them.[7]

Notes

Chapter 1

1. All names in this publication have been abbreviated to maintain confidentiality. This interviewee was classified 'coloured' under apartheid law. In this book all the authors use racial and ethnic classifications designed by the apartheid state. However, the problematic terminology is used in a critical fashion. The vast majority of interviewees also use these terms as a form of self-reference. All the interviews quoted in this chapter are from the Centre for Popular Memory's sound archives, which are kept in the Department of Manuscripts and Archives at the University of Cape Town.
2. Many more people were forcibly removed in South Africa, but according to the Chief Land Claims Commissioner, Advocate Wallace Mqogi, this is the number of people who will possibly benefit from restitution claims (1999).
3. This quote is from S. Field, 'The Power of Exclusion: Moving Memories from Windermere to the Cape Flats, 1920s–1990s' (University of Essex, 1996).
4. The dissemination of oral histories can occur through various media, such as books, radio, television and museum exhibitions. However, the written medium does the least justice to the term 'oral' in oral history. Nevertheless, given that this is a book, we are attempting to push the limits of the written medium through specific interpretations of the oral-to-written text and the inclusion of as many photographs as possible.
5. In the past few years several publications on the Truth and Reconciliation Commission (TRC) have appeared. For example, see W. James and L. van de Vijver (eds.), *After the TRC: Reflections on Truth and Reconciliation in South Africa* (Cape Town, 2000) and C. Villa-Vincencio and W. Verwoerd (eds.), *Looking Back/Reaching Forward: Reflections on the Truth and Reconciliation Commission of South Africa* (Cape Town and London, 2000).

Chapter 2

1. For an introduction to Cape slavery written for schools, see N. Worden, *The Chains that Bind Us* (Cambridge, 1985).
2. See A. Davids, 'The Words that Slaves Made: A Study of the Culture, Languages, Schools and Literacy of Slaves in Cape Town and Their Influence on the Development of Arabic-Afrikaans' (University of Cape Town, 1989).
3. See N. Worden, *The Chains that Bind Us*.
4. See C. Saunders, 'The Creation of Ndabeni: Urban Segregation and African Resistance in Cape Town', in *Studies in the History of Cape Town*, vol. 1 (1979), pp. 165-87.
5. See V. Bickford-Smith, *Ethnic Pride and Racial Prejudice in Victorian Cape Town* (Cambridge, 1995).
6. C. Saunders, 'The Creation of Ndabeni', p. 174.
7. *Cape Argus*, 25 May 1891.
8. C. Saunders, 'The Creation of Ndabeni', pp. 169-70.
9. See E. van Heyningen, 'Cape Town and the Plague of 1901', in *Studies in the History of Cape Town*, vol. 4 (1981), pp. 66-107; and V. Bickford-Smith, *Ethnic Pride and Racial Prejudice*, pp. 150-60.
10. See C. Saunders, 'From Ndabeni to Langa', in *Studies in the History of Cape Town*, vol. 1 (1979).
11. C. Saunders, 'The Creation of Ndabeni', pp. 177-8.
12. C. Saunders, 'The Creation of Ndabeni', p. 182.
13. *Cape Times*, 8 January 1936, quoted in C. Saunders, 'From Ndabeni to Langa', p. 197.
14. C. Saunders, 'The Creation of Ndabeni', p. 180.
15. D. Welsh, 'The Growth of Towns', in M. Wilson and L. Thompson (eds.), *The Oxford History of South Africa* (Oxford: Oxford University Press, 1975), p. 198.
16. C. Saunders, 'From Ndabeni to Langa', pp. 194-230.
17. See Y. Muthien, *State and Resistance in South Africa, 1939-1965* (Aldershot, 1994), pp. 49-58; B. Kinkead-Weekes, 'Africans in Cape Town: State Policy and Popular Resistance, 1936-1973' (University of Cape Town, 1992), pp. 97-105; and P. Ntantala, *A Life's Mosaic, The Autobiography of Phyllis Ntantala* (Cape Town, 1992), pp. 132-5.
18. *Cape Argus*, 27 March 1894.
19. J. Western, *Outcast Cape Town* (Cape Town, 1981), p. 56.
20. U. Mesthrie, ' "No Place in the World to Go" – Control by Permit: The First Phase of the Group Areas Act in Cape Town in the 1950s', in *Studies in the History of Cape Town*, vol. 7 (1994), p. 187.
21. J. Western, *Outcast Cape Town*, pp. 48-58.
22. See R. Edgar (ed.), *An African American in South Africa: The Travel Notes of Ralph J. Bunche* (Johannesburg, 1992), p. 59.

23. See P. Scott, 'Cape Town a Multi-Racial City', in *Geographical Journal*, 121 (1955), pp. 149-57; P. Ntantala, *A Life's Mosaic*, p. 136; B. Kinkead-Weekes, 'Africans in Cape Town', p. 19; and J. Western, *Outcast Cape Town*, pp. 47-57.
24. Cited in U. Mesthrie, 'Swallowing the Gnat after the Camel: The Fraserdale–Black River Group Area Proclamation of 1966 in Rondebosch' (University of Cape Town).
25. See V. Bickford-Smith, E. van Heyningen and N. Worden, *Cape Town in the Twentieth Century* (Cape Town, 1999), p. 187.
26. V. Bickford-Smith, *et al.*, *Cape Town in the Twentieth Century*, p. 174.
27. S. Field, 'The Power of Exclusion: Moving Memories from Windermere to the Cape Flats, 1920s–1990s' (University of Essex, 1996), p. 128.
28. C. Saunders, 'From Ndabeni to Langa', p. 210.
29. V. Bickford-Smith, *et al.*, *Cape Town in the Twentieth Century*, p. 175.
30. V. Bickford-Smith, *et al.*, *Cape Town in the Twentieth Century*, p. 182.
31. For a history of struggle at Crossroads, see J. Cole, *Crossroads. The Politics of Reform and Repression. 1976–1986* (Johannesburg, 1987).
32. G. Cook, 'Khayelitsha: New Settlement Forms in the Cape Peninsula', in D. Smith (ed.), *The Apartheid City and Beyond* (London, 1992), pp. 125-35; and J. Cole, *Crossroads*, pp. 71-82.

Chapter 3
1. Muthien, Y. 'Pass Controls and Resistance, Cape Town, 1939–1965' (Oxford, 1989), p. 56.
2. This chapter provides an historical sketch of what happened in Windermere. For a more detailed account of events and interpretations of memory and identity in Windermere, see S. Field, 'The Power of Exclusion: Moving Memories from Windermere to the Cape Flats, 1920s–1990s' (University of Essex, 1996).
3. All interviews were conducted by the author in Cape Town during 1993. A Mr S.F. assisted with some of the African interviews. Note that some of these interviews and secondary quotes were also used in S. Field, 'The Power of Exclusion'.
4. Cape Town Files, South African Archives, 2 February 1923.
5. The section between 13th and 18th Avenues later became known as Factreton. The sub-economic housing estate of Factreton of today was built in stages from the 1950s to the late 1960s.
6. *Cape Times*, 26 May 1946.
7. S. Field, 'The Power of Exclusion', p. 156.
8. *Cape Times*, 15 May 1943.
9. Y. Muthien, 'Pass Controls and Resistance', p. 59.

10. *Cape Times*, 6 January 1951.
11. SHAWCO stands for the Student Health and Welfare Centres Organisation and has its head office in 12th Avenue, Kensington.
12. *Cape Argus*, 1 March 1944.
13. M. Horrell, *The Pass Laws, A Fact Paper*, No. 7 (Cape Town, 1960), p. 2.
14. Y. Muthien, 'Pass Controls and Resistance', p. 47.
15. B. Kinkead-Weekes, 'Africans in Cape Town: The Origins and Development of State Policy and Popular Resistance, 1936–1973' (University of Cape Town, 1992), p. 338.
16. *Cape Argus*, 9 September 1953.
17. *Cape Times*, 25 February 1948.
18. *Cape Times*, 2 August 1955.
19. Western Cape Administration Board Files, South African Archives, Mr Geddie, letter dated 18 January 1961.
20. *Cape Times*, 26 November 1955.
21. For a detailed discussion of the Nyanga transit camp and the housing developments in the area, see H. Fast, 'Pondoks, Houses and Hostels: A History of Nyanga, 1946–1970, with a Special Focus on Housing' (University of Cape Town, 1995).
22. The common 'blood' story is a powerful myth that helped many people to make sense of the madness of apartheid and to carry on despite the harsh realities. For a detailed discussion of myth and memory, see R. Samuel and P. Thompson, *The Myths We Live By* (London, 1990).
23. *New Age*, 5 May 1955.
24. *Cape Times*, 11 September 1958.
25. *Cape Argus*, 25 October 1963.
26. There were exceptions: a few African individuals managed to illegally reclassify themselves as coloured in order to remain in the area. See the stories from Mr D.S. in S. Field, 'The Power of Exclusion', pp. 96-8.

Chapter 4
1. This quote is from an interview with Mr E.C. All interviews were conducted by the author as part of her Ph.D. thesis research.
2. See S. Patterson, *Colour and Culture in South Africa* (London, 1953).
3. *Cape Argus*, 14 September 1961.
4. For Lawrence, see Juta's *Cape Town and Suburban Directory 1898*; for Paulsen and Weppenaar, see Juta's *Cape Town Suburban Directory 1901*. Also see the Marriage Record, 1875–1903, and the Baptism Record, 1873–1901 and 1895–1905, of St James Church, Green Point. See Juta's *Cape Town Suburban Directory 1903* and *Cape Times*, 16 October 1959, for Parker.

5. *Cape Argus*, 23 September 1959. An article in the *Cape Times* of 23 September 1959 reports that more than three hundred people lived in Tramway Road and Ilford Street.

6. *Cape Times*, 23 September 1959.

7. See V. Bickford-Smith, *Ethnic Pride and Racial Prejudice in Victorian Cape Town* (Cambridge, 1995).

8. See M. Weber, *Economy and Society*, in G. Ross and C. Wittich (eds.), vol. 3 (New York, 1963), on status and power.

9. Bickford-Smith *et al.*, *Cape Town in the Twentieth Century* (Cape Town, 1999), p. 172.

10. *New Age*, 12 November 1959.

11. Letters addressed to Mr J. Arendse of Number 25 Tramway Road Cottages and Mr C. Paulsen of Number 2 Tramway Road Cottages are examples of such correspondence.

12. *Cape Times*, 26 September 1959.

13. *Cape Argus*, 23 September 1959, and *Cape Times*, 23 September 1959.

14. *Cape Times*, 7 November 1959.

15. *Cape Argus*, 15 June 1963.

16. Mr L.L. during a conversation with officials from the Department of Land Restitution, 1997. 'Casspirs' refers to armoured police vehicles.

17. *Sunday Times*, 7 November 1999.

Chapter 5

1. This article was compiled from interviews in the Western Cape Oral History Project (WCOHP) sound archive, District Six Collection.

2. B. Barrow, quoted in C. Schoeman, *District Six: The Spirit of Kanaladorp* (Cape Town, 1994), p. 43.

3. B. Nasson, 'Oral History and the Reconstruction of District Six', in S. Jeppie and C. Soudien (eds.), *The Struggle for District Six: Past and Present* (Cape Town, 1990), p. 123.

4. *Cape Times*, 8 March 1966, quoted in S. Jeppie and C. Soudien (eds.), *The Struggle for District Six*, p. 123.

5. Conversation with Mr V.K., April 1998.

6. G. Abraham-Willis, South African Cultural Museum Newsletter, 1997.

7. D. Warren, 'The Early Years of District Six: District Twelve in the 1840s', in *Cabo* 3(4), 1985.

8. See V. Bickford-Smith, 'The Origins and Early History of District Six to 1910', in *Cabo* 4(2), 1987.

9. V. Bickford-Smith, 'The Origins and Early History of District Six' in S. Jeppie and C. Soudien (eds.), *The Struggle for District Six*, p. 36.

10. C. Schoeman, *District Six: The Spirit of Kanaladorp*, p. 17.

11. N. Barnett, 'The Planned Destruction of District Six in 1949' (Cape Town, 1991), p. 8.

12. Quoted in N. Barnett, 'The Planned Destruction of District Six', p. 5.

13. N. Barnett, 'The Planned Destruction of District Six', p. 2.

14. N. Barnett, 'The Planned Destruction of District Six', p. 2.

15. K. McCormick, 'The Vernacular of District Six', in S. Jeppie and C. Soudien (eds.), *The Struggle for District Six*, pp. 108-9.

16. L. Fortune, *The House on Tyne Street: Childhood Memories of District Six* (Cape Town, 1996), p. 84.

17. B. Barrow, quoted in C. Schoeman, *District Six: The Spirit of Kanaladorp*, p. 35.

18. A. La Guma, quoted in D. Hart, 'Political Manipulation of Urban Space: The Razing of District Six, Cape Town', in S. Jeppie and C. Soudien (eds.), *The Struggle for District Six*, p. 122.

19. L. Fortune, *The House on Tyne Street*, p. 64.

20. Mr W., quoted in B. Nasson, 'Oral History and the Reconstruction of District Six', in S. Jeppie and C. Soudien (eds.), *The Struggle for District Six*, p. 56.

21. D. Hart, 'Political Manipulation of Urban Space', in S. Jeppie and C. Soudien (eds.), *The Struggle for District Six*, p. 121.

22. L. Fortune, *The House on Tyne Street*, pp. 4-8.

23. N. Ngcelwane, *Sala Kahle, District Six: An African Women's Perspective* (Cape Town, 1998), p. 15.

24. N. Ngcelwane, *Sala Kahle, District Six*, p. 21.

25. D. Pinnock, *The Brotherhoods: Street Gangs and State Control in Cape Town* (Cape Town, 1984), pp. 107-8.

26. C. Schoeman, *District Six: The Spirit of Kanaladorp*, p. 47.

27. See B. Nasson, 'She Preferred Living in a Cave with Harry the Snake-Catcher: Towards an Oral History of Popular Leisure and Class Expression in District Six, Cape Town, circa 1920s–1950s' (Johannesburg, 1987).

28. L. Fortune, *The House on Tyne Street*, p. 82.

29. L. Fortune, *The House on Tyne Street*, p. 82.

30. N. Ngcelwane, *Sala Kahle, District Six*, p. 43.

31. Quoted in B. Nasson, 'Oral History and the Reconstruction of District Six', in S. Jeppie and C. Soudien (eds.), *The Struggle for District Six*, p. 59.

32. See B. Nasson, 'She Preferred Living in a Cave'.

33. V. Bickford-Smith, *Ethnic Pride and Racial Prejudice in Victorian Cape Town* (Cambridge, 1995), p. 188.

34. A. Davids, quoted in C. Schoeman, *District Six: The Spirit of Kanaladorp*, p. 43.

35. N. Ngcelwane, *Sala Kahle, District Six*, p. 67.

36. 'Boere' is a derogatory term referring to white Afrikaners or policemen.

37. 'Hotnots' is an abbreviation of the word 'Hottentots' and a derogatory term referring to coloured people.

38. V. Bickford-Smith *et al.*, *Cape Town in the Twentieth Century* (Cape Town, 1999), p. 73.

39. S. Field, 'From the "Peaceful Past" to the "Violent Present": Memory, Myth and Identity in Guguletu', in D. Howarth and A. Norval (eds.), *South Africa in Transition: New Theoretical Perspectives* (London, 1998), p. 73.

40. Conversation with Mr V.K., April 1998.

41. S. Field, 'From the "Peaceful Past" to the "Violent Present"', p. 75.

42. See C. Saunders, 'The Struggle for District Six in the Context of Urban History in South Africa', in *Studies in the History of Cape Town*, vol. 3 (1980).

43. R. Rive, 'District Six: Fact and Fiction', in S. Jeppie and C. Soudien (eds.), *The Struggle for District Six*, pp. 110-16.

Chapter 6

1. This quote is by Mr. A.Am. This paper is based on an oral history project conducted by the author in 1995. All the quotations are from interviews that can be found in the Western Cape Oral History Project sound archive.

2. B.B. Brock and B.G. Willis, *Historical Simon's Town* (Cape Town, 1976), p. 3.

3. Interviewees were drawn from the wealthy and the poor and include a teacher, a former school principal, working-class artisans and labourers, and members of the Christian as well as Islamic faiths. Twenty-four people were interviewed, two representatives from each area of greater Simon's Town. All were over the age of 60 years and thus could recall their childhood, youth and married life in Simon's Town, as well as subsequent removals. Tenants and landowners who were forced to move to Ocean View and those moved to other coloured suburbs such as Heathfield, Retreat and Grassy Park were interviewed.

4. B.B. Brock and B.G. Willis, *Historical Simon's Town*, p. 13. A flute was a typical round-sterned, ship-rigged Dutch merchant ship of this period designed to carry the largest possible cargo with the smallest possible crew.

5. In Simon's Town, the African community of Luyolo heeded the call of the Pan-Africanist Congress in 1960 to march on police stations and to burn their pass books.

6. White Paper A-56: Exchange of Letters in Defence Matters between the Government of the Union of South Africa and the United Kingdom, Government Printers, Pretoria, 1956. It is also generally known as the Simon's Town Agreement.

7. The Jaffa family was given the rights to trek at Kleinvishoek because the extension of the Naval Dockyard had swallowed up 'Jaffa's Beach' and the Breda family had ceased trekking there for many years. The Jaffa family moved to Mitchells Plain and it became very difficult for them to travel to Simon's Town daily. After a while the trekking rights were passed on to Mr Suleiman Aghmat of Ocean View.

8. My father began working at the Naval Dockyard in 1940 as a skilled labourer. When he finally left in 1946, he was an experienced electrical wireman, a technically skilled job, which was reserved for white males at that time.

9. Mr L.C. still lives in Ocean View today.

10. One of my interviewees, Mr. K.H., showed me a picture of his grandfather as the 'Worthy Master' of the Simon's Town Chapter of the Freemasons with all the other members. His grandfather was Scottish and came from England to work in the Naval Dockyard towards the end of the nineteenth century.

11. For further discussion of the social position and boundaries of people classified coloured under apartheid, see H. Dickie-Clark, *The Marginal Situation: A Sociological Study of the Coloured Group* (London, 1966), and M. Whisson, *The Fairest Cape: An Account of the Coloured People of the District of Simon's Town* (Johannesburg, 1974).

12. When Mrs T.F. telephoned me a day later to relate how her husband lost his job in the Dockyard, the tape recorder unfortunately did not function properly. I had to reconstruct this from memory, with the approval of Mrs T.F.

13. This was stated at the public enquiries of 1959 held in Simon's Town, found in verbatim notes taken by B. Willis, 'Public Enquiries of the Group Areas Board', in a special drawer at the Simon's Town Museum.

14. B. Willis, 'Preliminary Information for Those Affected by the Group Areas Proclamations', February 1968, Simon's Town, Simon's Town Museum.

15. The name 'Slangkop' was taken from Slangkop Point nearby. It was dropped after a few years, when the Housing Office held a survey and people selected the name Ocean View for the township from three names offered.

16. B. Willis, 'Preliminary Information'.

17. B. Willis, 'Preliminary Information'.

18. B. Willis, 'Preliminary Information'.

19. B. Willis, 'Preliminary Information'.

20. Mrs L. was not one of my interviewees. She passed on this information recently.

21. S. Field, 'Fragile Identities: Stories of Coloured

Residents of the Cape Flats', in Z. Erasmus and
E. Pieterse (eds.), *Coloured by History, Shaped by
Place*, forthcoming.

22. I. Goldin, *Making Race: The Politics and Economics of
Coloured Identity in South Africa* (London, 1987),
p. xiii.

23. I. Goldin, *Making Race*, p. xiv.

24. See also G. Lewis, *Between the Wire and the Wall: A
History of South African Coloured Politics* (Cape
Town, 1987).

25. Throughout this chapter I have used the statutory
classification 'coloured', a term widely rejected by
the people it is supposed to define.

Chapter 7

1. See United Women's Organisation. *Claremont: A
People's History* (Athlone).

2. This chapter is based on a series of interviews conducted by Karen Daniels in 1994 which form part
of the Western Cape Oral History Project sound
archive. Interviews from the Coon Carnival
Collection by Lisa Baxter and from the District Six
Collection have also been included.

3. *Cape Argus*, 18 November 1969.

4. *Cape Times*, 19 November 1969.

5. J. Murray, *Claremont Album*, p. 46.

6. W. Taliep, 'A Study in the History of Claremont
and the Impact of the Group Areas Act, circa
1950–1970' (Cape Town, 1992), p. 2.

7. L. Thomas, *St Matthews Church, Claremont: A
Glimpse into the Past One Hundred Years* (Claremont,
1993), pp. 1-2.

8. F.J. Pearce, *Souvenir of Claremont: 1882–1907*, p. 6.

9. W. Taliep, 'A Study in the History of Claremont',
p. 2.

10. Interview with Mr R.D., in W. Taliep, 'A Study in
History of Claremont'.

11. United Women's Organisation, *Claremont: A People's
History*, p. 7.

12. *Southern Suburbs Tatler*, 24 June 1999.

13. U. Mesthrie, ' "No Place in the World to Go" –
Control by Permit: The First Phase of the Group
Areas Act in Cape Town in the 1950s', in *Studies in
the History of Cape Town*, vol. 7 (1994)', p. 15.

14. *Cape Times*, 19 November 1969.

15. *Cape Argus*, 18 November 1969.

16. United Women's Organisation, *Claremont: A People's
History*, pp. 14-21.

17. *Southern Suburbs Tatler*, 24 June 1999.

18. Interview with Mr R.D., in W. Taliep, 'A Study in
the History Of Claremont'.

19. United Women's Organisation, *Claremont: A People's
History*, pp. 17-21.

20. Interview with Mr R.D., in W. Taliep, 'A Study in
the History of Claremont', Appendix.

21. United Women's Organisation, *Claremont: A People's
History*, p. 14.

Chapter 8

1. This quote by Mrs S.D. is from an interview with
S. Field.

2. For examples of different approaches to oral
history see R. Perks and A. Thomson (eds.),
The Oral History Reader (London, 1998), and
D. Dunaway and W.K. Baum (eds.), *Oral History,
An Interdisciplinary Anthology*, 2nd ed. (Walnut
Creek, 1996).

3. This programme has three key elements: the
restitution of land rights to the survivors of forced
removals, land tenure reform, and land redistribu-
tion in order to address imbalances caused by
racially skewed land distribution.

4. A. du Toit, 'Land Restitution, Policy and
Implementation' (1998), p. 34.

5. This right also refers to labour tenants, share-
croppers, customary law interests, and beneficiaries
under a trust.

6. H. Barnes, 'Land Reform in South Africa' (Cape
Town, 1997), p. 7.

7. Rather, land claims are based on the length of
occupation, customary notions of birthright and
expectations of secure tenure based on consensual
practices. See N. Murphy, 'The Restitution of Land
after Apartheid: The Constitutional and Legislative
Framework', in M. Rwelamira and G. Werle (eds.),
Confronting Past Injustices (Durban, 1996), p. 116.

8. For example, under the Group Areas Act of 1950
the state identified 'disqualified persons' without
title who were forced to leave, but record was only
kept of 'heads of households'. See A. du Toit, 'Land
Restitution', p. 56.

9. The information below was provided by staff members of the Commission for Land Rights and
Restitution as of 28 January 2000. The
Commission is still in the process of organising its
database according to community areas; therefore
these figures should be treated with caution. It has
also been impossible to get a precise breakdown
for the different categories of claimants, such as
property owners, tenants and businesses.

10. *Sunday Times Metro*, 7 November 1999. About
forty to forty-five families are due to return; the
rest have claimed compensation.

11. This figure includes 387 claims from the Luyolo
township. Mr Albert Thomas, a member of this
committee, says the total number of claims for
Simon's Town is actually over a thousand.

12. This figure includes claims for lower and upper
Claremont. The Commission was unsure whether
this committee was still functioning.

13. These figures are also from the Commission and are as of 28 January 2000. Note that sometimes a 'claim' might apply to only one tenant or property owner, but in other cases it might apply to several hundred beneficiaries.

14. *Sunday Times Metro*, 7 November 1999.

15. Mrs S.D. in an interview with S. Field.

16. N. Ebrahim, *Noor's Story. My Life in District Six* (Cape Town, 1999), p. 83.

17. J. Bornat, 'Oral History as a Social Movement: Reminiscence and Older People', in R. Perks and A. Thomson (eds.), *The Oral History Reader* (London, 1998), p. 189.

18. Quoted in D. Skinner, *Apartheid's Violent Legacy, A Report on Trauma in the Western Cape* (Cape Town, 1998), p. 147.

19. During the Truth and Reconciliation Commission (TRC) hearings, the issue of emotional healing was often framed in terms of a medical discourse. Put bluntly, the healing of emotional wounds is not a matter that is resolved by going to a doctor and receiving medication. The emotional healing of a traumatic experience like forced removals and other apartheid experiences will take decades. Sadly, for many people the healing will never be complete.

20. N. Cross and R. Barker, 'The SAHEL Oral History Project', in R. Perks and A. Thomson (eds.), *The Oral History Reader* (London, 1998), p. 257.

21. See N. Ngcelwane, *Sala Kahle, District Six: An African Women's Perspective* (Cape Town, 1998), p. 9.

Appendix

1. Oral traditions refer to oral stories that are passed on from generation to generation. Oral history refers to the lived practice of talking about the past, and to the research practice of interviewing people. For a detailed discussion of the differences between oral tradition and oral history, read J. Vansina, *Oral Tradition as History*, 2nd ed. (London, 1985).

2. This is not a comprehensive list or description. Those who want to learn more about oral history research methodology should read P. Thompson, *The Voice of the Past, Oral History*, 2nd ed. (Oxford, 1988).

3. Note that there are many recent technological innovations. For example, digital sound can be played through specific computer software programmes that transcribe the sound into written text.

4. For excellent ideas on the methods and interpretations of oral histories, see A. Portelli, *The Death of Luigi Trastulli and Other Stories, Form and Meaning in Oral History* (New York, 1991); and R. Perks and A. Thomson (eds.), *The Oral History Reader* (London, 1998).

5. The third option is to employ an interviewer who can speak the interviewee's first language to conduct the interview. However, the common drawback of this option is that the interviewer usually does not have the depth of research knowledge that the primary researcher should have. Conversely, an advantage of using a fieldworker is that he or she may be more aware of specific local knowledge forms and practices than the primary researcher.

6. Other important details are the title of the project and the duration of the interview. If you are doing several interviews, develop a clear numbering system.

7. For further discussion on using oral history as a form of public history presented through different mediums, see D. Ritchie, *Doing Oral History* (New York, 1995).

Bibliography

Barnes, H. 'Land Reform in South Africa.' (University of Cape Town: Unpublished Seminar Paper, 1997)

Barnett, N. 'The Planned Destruction of District Six in 1949.' (University of Cape Town: Cape Town History Project Paper, 1991)

Bickford-Smith, V. *Ethnic Pride and Racial Prejudice in Victorian Cape Town*. (Cambridge: Cambridge University Press, 1995)

Bickford-Smith, V. 'The Origins and Early History of District Six to 1910', in *Cabo* 4(2), 1987

Bickford-Smith, V., Van Heyningen, E. and Worden, N. *Cape Town in the Twentieth Century*. (Cape Town: David Philip, 1999)

Bornat, J. 'Oral History as a Social Movement: Reminiscence and Older People', in R. Perks and A. Thomson (eds.), *The Oral History Reader*. (London: Routledge, 1998)

Brock, B.B. and Willis, B.G. (eds.). *Historical Simon's Town*. (Cape Town: A.A. Balkema, 1976)

Cole, J. *Crossroads. The Politics of Reform and Repression. 1976–1986*. (Johannesburg: Ravan Press, 1987)

Cook, G. 'Khayelitsha: New Settlement Forms in the Cape Peninsula', in D. Smith (ed.), *The Apartheid City and Beyond*. (London: Routledge, 1992)

Cross, N. and Barker, R. 'The SAHEL Oral History Project', in R. Perks and A. Thomson (eds.), *The Oral History Reader*. (London: Routledge, 1998)

Davids, A. 'The Words that Slaves Made: A Study of the Culture, Languages, Schools and Literacy of Slaves in Cape Town and Their Influence on the Development of Arabic–Afrikaans.' (University of Cape Town: Unpublished History Department Seminar Paper, 1989)

Dickie-Clarke, H.F. *The Marginal Situation: A Sociological Study of the Coloured Group*. (London: Routledge and Kegan Paul, 1966)

du Toit, A. 'Land Restitution, Policy and Implementation.' (Department of Land Affairs: Unpublished Course Handbook, 1998)

Dunaway, D. and Baum, W.K. (eds.). *Oral History, An Interdisciplinary Anthology*. 2nd ed. (Walnut Creek: Altamira Press, 1996)

Ebrahim, N. *Noor's Story. My Life in District Six*. (Cape Town: The District Six Museum Foundation, 1999)

Edgar, R. (ed.). *An African American in South Africa: The Travel Notes of Ralph J. Bunche*. (Johannesburg: University of Witwatersrand Press, 1992)

Fast, H. 'Pondoks, Houses and Hostels: A History of Nyanga, 1946–1970, with a Special Focus on Housing.' (University of Cape Town: Unpublished Ph.D. Thesis, 1995)

Field, S. 'From the "Peaceful Past" to the "Violent Present": Memory, Myth and Identity in Guguletu', in D. Howarth and A. Norval (eds.), *South Africa in Transition: New Theoretical Perspectives*. (London: Macmillan Press, 1998)

Field, S. 'The Power of Exclusion: Moving Memories from Windermere to the Cape Flats, 1920s–1990s.' (University of Essex: Unpublished Ph.D. Thesis, 1996)

Fortune, L. *The House on Tyne Street: Childhood Memories of District Six*. (Cape Town: Kwela Books, 1996)

Goldin, I. *Making Race: The Politics and Economics of Coloured Identity in South Africa*. (London: Maskew Miller Longman, 1987)

Horrel, M. *The Pass Laws, A Fact Paper*, No. 7 (Cape Town: South African Institute for Race Relations, 1960)

James, W. and Van de Vijver, L. (eds.). *After the TRC: Reflections on Truth and Reconciliation in South Africa*. (Cape Town: David Philip, 2000)

Jeppie, S. and Soudien, C. (eds.). *The Struggle for District Six: Past and Present*. (Cape Town: Buchu Books, 1990)

Kinkead-Weekes, B. 'Africans in Cape Town: The Origins and Development of State Policy and Popular Resistance, 1936–1973.' (University of Cape Town: Unpublished Ph.D. Thesis, 1992)

Lewis, G. *Between the Wire and the Wall: A History of South African Coloured Politics*. (Cape Town: David Philip, 1987)

Mesthrie, U. '"No Place in the World to Go" – Control by Permit: The First Phase of the Group Areas Act in Cape Town in the 1950s', in *Studies in the History of Cape Town*, vol. 7 (1994)

Mesthrie, U. 'Swallowing the Gnat after the Camel: The Fraserdale–Black River Group Area Proclamation of 1966 in Rondebosch.' (University of Cape Town: Unpublished Seminar Paper)

Mqogi, W. 'The New Approach to Land Claims, The Administrative Approach and the Role of the Land Claims Court.' (Department of Land Affairs: Discussion Document, 1999)

Murphy, N. 'The Restitution of Land after Apartheid: The Constitutional and Legislative Framework', in

M. Rwelamira and G. Werle (eds.), *Confronting Past Injustices.* (Durban: Butterworths, 1996)

Murray, J. *Claremont Album.*

Muthien, Y. 'Pass Controls and Resistance, Cape Town, 1939–1965.' (Oxford University: Unpublished Ph.D. Thesis, 1989)

Muthien, Y. *State and Resistance in South Africa, 1939–1965.* (Aldershot: Ashgate Publishing, 1994)

Nasson, B. 'She Preferred Living in a Cave with Harry the Snake-Catcher: Towards an Oral History of Popular Leisure and Class Expression in District Six, Cape Town, circa 1920s–1950s.' (University of the Witwatersrand: History Workshop, 1987)

Ngcelwane, N. *Sala Kahle, District Six: An African Women's Perspective.* (Cape Town: Kwela Books, 1998)

Ntantala, P. *A Life's Mosaic, The Autobiography of Phyllis Ntantala.* (Cape Town: David Philip, 1992)

Patterson, S. *Colour and Culture in South Africa.* (London: Routledge and Kegan Paul, 1953)

Pearce, F.J. *Souvenir of Claremont: 1882–1907.*

Perks, R. and Thomson, A. (eds.). *The Oral History Reader.* (London: Routledge, 1998)

Pinnock, D. *The Brotherhoods: Street Gangs and State Control in Cape Town.* (Cape Town: David Philip, 1984)

Portelli, A. *The Death of Luigi Trastulli and Other Stories, Form and Meaning in Oral History.* (New York: State University of New York Press, 1991)

Ritchie, D. *Doing Oral History.* (New York: Twayne Publishers, 1995)

Samuel, R. and Thompson, P. *The Myths We Live By.* (London: Routledge, 1990)

Saunders, C. 'From Ndabeni to Langa', in *Studies in the History of Cape Town*, vol. 1 (1979).

Saunders, C. 'The Creation of Ndabeni: Urban Segregation and African Resistance in Cape Town', in *Studies in the History of Cape Town*, vol. 1 (1979)

Saunders, C. 'The Struggle for District Six in the Context of Urban History in South Africa', in *Studies in the History of Cape Town*, vol. 3 (1980)

Schoeman, C. *District Six: The Spirit of Kanaladorp.* (Cape Town: Human and Rousseau, 1994)

Scott, P. 'Cape Town a Multi-Racial City', in *Geographical Journal*, 121 (1955).

Skinner, D. *Apartheid's Violent Legacy, A Report on Trauma in the Western Cape.* (Cape Town: The Trauma Centre for Victims of Violence and Torture, 1998)

Taliep, W. 'A Study in the History of Claremont and the Impact of the Group Areas Act, circa 1950–1970.' (University of Cape Town: Unpublished Honours Thesis, 1992)

Thomas, L. *St Matthews Church, Claremont: A Glimpse into the Past One Hundred Years.* (Claremont, 1993)

Thompson, P. *The Voice of the Past, Oral History.* 2nd ed. (Oxford: Oxford University Press, 1988)

United Women's Organisation. *Claremont: A People's History.* (Athlone: UWO Claremont Branch)

van Heyningen, E. 'Cape Town and the Plague of 1901', in *Studies in the History of Cape Town*, vol. 4 (1981)

Vansina, J. *Oral Tradition as History.* 2nd ed. (London: James Currey, 1985)

Villa-Vincencio, C. and Verwoerd, W. (eds.). *Looking Back/Reaching Forward: Reflections on the Truth and Reconciliation Commission of South Africa.* (Cape Town and London: University of Cape Town Press, 2000)

Warren, D. 'The Early Years of District Six: District Twelve in the 1840s', in *Cabo* 3(4), 1985

Weber, M. *Economy and Society*, in G. Ross and C. Wittich (eds.), vol. 3 (New York: Bedminister Press, 1963)

Welsh, D. 'The Growth of Towns', in M. Wilson and L. Thompson (eds.), *The Oxford History of South Africa.* (Oxford: Oxford University Press, 1975)

Western, J. *Outcast Cape Town.* (Cape Town: George Allen and Unwin, 1981)

Whisson, M.G. *The Fairest Cape: An Account of the Coloured People of the District of Simon's Town.* (Johannesburg: Institute of Race Relations, 1974)

Worden, N. *The Chains that Bind Us.* (Cambridge: Cambridge University Press, 1985)

Index